JESUS CIRCLES

JESUS CIRCLES

A Way to Heal Our Wounds,

Subvert the Domination System,

and Build an Abundant Future

Peter R. Lawson

Library of Congress Number: 2003099094
ISBN :   Hardcover   1-4134-4085-1
                Softcover   1-4134-4084-3

This book was printed in the United States of America.

Bible quotations are from the New Revised Standard Version Bible, copyright 1989, Division of Christian Education of the National Council of the Churches of Christ in the United States of America. Used by permission. All rights reserved.

To order additional copies of this book, contact:
Xlibris Corporation
1-888-795-4274
www.Xlibris.com
Orders@Xlibris.com
20202

Dedication

To my Grandmother Sallie,
who set the pattern by believing that a parent's job was
to blow gently into flame the tiny spark of a child's unique spirit
without blowing so hard as to extinguish it forever.

To my parents Ray and Alice,
conservative Republicans who raised me in a non-violent household
and whose capacity for risk gave me the liberty to be a radical.

To my children and grandchildren
whose lives grace the universe
and carry on the tradition.

To my beloved wife, Danielle,
who knows better than anyone
what a wicked nincompoop I am
and loves me nevertheless.

CONTENTS

Glossary 11

Prelude: The Jesus Assembly of Santa Clarita, Sunday,
            April 3, 2007 15

Introduction 21

Chapter 1: How I Got to Three Foundational Perceptions: Jesus,
            the Itinerant Visionary Sage,
            the Circle Process,
            and the Domination System 30

Chapter 2: The Domination System Then and Now 44

Chapter 3: The Once Rural Agrarian and the Now Urban,
            Postindustrial Culture 52

Interlude   72

Chapter 4: Jesus: the Work of an Itinerant Sage 74

Chapter 5: Why Jesus Circles Today? 84

Interlude   97

Chapter 6: The Circle Process in Detail 100

Chapter 7: Designing the Circle Process for
            Large Assemblies 117

Chapter 8: Getting Deeper into the Way of Jesus:
            Some Session Topics 122

Appendix 1: Old Testament Violence 133

Appendix 2: New Testament Violence 138

Appendix 3: On African Bible Study 142

Bibliography 145

Postscript   153

If you can check off any two of the following statements, this book may be for you.

- I am seeking an authentic way to walk with courage into the uncertainties of the third millennium.
- How can I live abundantly in the midst of the domination systems that are death dealing, violent, unjust, and sometimes very painful?
- I have passed beyond traditional religion.
- The traditional notions of God don't match my reality.
- How can I learn to live in a permanent state of uncertainty?
- I am tired of violence and want to be a peacemaker.
- I have difficulty accepting traditional theology.
- I see so much injustice and want to help make the world be different.
- Until recently I called myself a Christian and have now dissociated myself from traditional, evangelical, or fundamental churches.
- I am impaled on Jesus, and I can't seem to avoid his call to live in a new way.
- How can I be a part of the worldwide communities working to bring about a New Human Being and a New Human Society?
- I am in love with Jesus, but not his followers.
- I have concluded that contemporary religious organizations are, by and large, dysfunctional, codependent, death dealing, highly political, bureaucratic, patriarchal, literalistic

organizations which are now dying and, therefore, fundamentally oriented toward institutional survival.

* I have encountered the new Jesus and found an energizing relationship with his dynamic charisma and cannot find a nurturing fellowship.

* I am seeking ways of adapting the teaching of Jesus to the realities of the postmodern era.

GLOSSARY

Abundance—It is used in this book to signify a total way of being in the world. Abundance is a fundamental social, economic, and political matter. It is first about distributive justice. More than that, it is fulness of life in all its dimensions. Humans cannot fully appropriate the beauty and delight of the abundant natural world until their basic needs of adequate food, clothing, and shelter are met.

Basilea—In the King James New Testament the Greek *Basileia* is translated as "kingdom." A more accurate translation is "empire." When Jesus says, "The *Basileia* of God is like . . .," he is setting up the idea of an Empire of God in contrast to the Roman Empire.

> Hal Taussig has suggested that we use a modern term to designate the contemporary manifestations of empire. How about "multinational corporation," "multinational business community," "the global free market economy," or "multinational conglomerate"? What would you think of "the culture of violence"?

Distributive justice—Distributive justice is different from criminal, racial, or retributive justice. It means that the assets, benefits, and gifts of the natural world, whether that be lumber, wheat, or diamonds, are the possession of all people everywhere and are to be shared out as equitably as possible. A system of distributive justice is egalitarian and seeks abundance for every human on the planet. Criminal, racial, and retributive justice are manifestations of the culture of violence.

Domain—A sphere of activity, concern, or function; a field: the domain of history; or a cluster of institutions.

Domain of God—a way of saying kingdom of God while minimizing the "royal" connotations. Based on the definition of domain as a territory over which rule or control is exercised.

Domination system—a hierarchical social system in which the elites exercise power backed by violence to maximize their wealth by exploiting those beneath them in the hierarchy.

Elites—those individuals and families at the top of the social structure in the domination system; those who reap the benefits and control the wealth and productivity of society.

Empire of God—another way of translating *basileia tou theou.*

Kingdom of God—the way the translators of the King James Version translated the Greek *basileia tou theou.*

New Human Being—is the term I use for the society that can emerge when the culture of violence disappears. It also applies to those folks who are living as nonviolent peacemakers here and now.

Polity—The form of government of a nation, state, church, or organization.

Syndic—is the term I use for those chosen to represent their small circle in a large assembly circle.

The Way or Jesus' Way—the journey to a way of life modeled on the teaching and program of the historical Jesus.

Vigilante—One who takes or advocates the taking of law enforcement into one's own hands. A member of a vigilance committee.

Wisdom Keeper—the person who is responsible for the process of the circle (and perhaps makes the final decision).

PRELUDE

The Jesus Assembly of Santa Clarita, Sunday, April 3, 2007

It's just before ten o'clock in the morning when Sarah Robertson leans her bike on the side of the old Mesa Grande Schoolhouse, climbs the steps, and unlocks the doors. The school itself has been closed for several years, but its two rooms are rented out on a regular basis for private parties, art shows, and community events. Every first Sunday of the month it is rented to the Santa Clarita Assembly of the Galilean Sage, or as some calls it, the Jesus Assembly. Although Sarah is only a teenager, seventeen to be exact, she was selected by lot to be the Wisdom Keeper for this Sunday. She came early to be prepared. Sarah has aired out the room and cleaned up a bit in anticipation of the arrival of her folks, her friends, and sometimes, it seems, her extended family. Now she watches the cars and vans pulling into the school parking lot. Most of the arrivals she knows very well, and as usual there are a number of strangers.

This assembly has been meeting once a month for nearly six years. It is like a church, but it is not a church. It has none of the marks usually associated with a church and its congregation.

In the first place it only meets once a month. There is no church building. The Mesa Grande Schoolhouse is the third of the rented venues they have used. There are no clergy or ministers. It is an organization without a president, or officers of any kind. It has no board of trustees. They don't take up an offering. In fact, they have no budget, no checking account, and they are not registered with the state or the IRS as a nonprofit institution.

It is a diverse group of people of all ages, dress, colors, and countries of origin who are moving from their cars into the schoolhouse. As they come in, one notices that many of them are carrying covered dishes and coolers; some with pie plates and some with crock pots. Some carry nothing at all. Inside, the tables to either side of the room are being covered with food containers. In the middle of the room there is an inner circle of twelve chairs and a seemingly haphazard arrangement of chairs behind them. Several people move in and sit in the inner circle. Others sit in the chairs surrounding that inner circle. In the very center is a Tibetan singing bowl and its felt-covered striker.

In a few moments all twelve chairs of the inner circle are occupied, and Sarah rises from her seat in the inner circle, moves to the center, and circles the singing bowl to make it sing and then strikes the bowl. As it resonates, the room becomes very quiet. She moves again to the center and strikes the singing bowl again. When its last vibration disappears, the girl says, "We are gathered in our April Jesus Circle, to search out the wisdom we need for these days. I ask that we wait silently for a minute and quiet our hearts and minds to be fully present to one another here and now. And may the spirit of the living Jesus empower us."

The preparatory silence is broken when Sarah recalls to everyone the basic norms of the circle process that the assembly will use today as it has for all the years of its life. Today she emphasizes the need for everyone to offer their wisdom to the singing bowl in the center. It is if, she says, they are placing their personal wisdom in the bowl. She reminds them that at the end of the circle session they will offer the contents of their wisdom up as a prayer for the life of the world.

She concludes, "Let's begin with check-in." Then she tells the group about her anxiety over being the Wisdom Keeper for the first time. Sarah describes her struggles over the last two months to focus on her task today and her prayers for the calm and grace to fulfill her role well for the benefit of the whole assembly.

As she ends her remarks she touches the shoulder of the sixty-year-old man sitting to the left. He reports, quite simply, that he has had one of the most joyful months he can remember. He touches the shoulder of the forty-four-year-old woman to his left. And around the circle, each of the twelve reports in on the events of the past month. Each of them, while speaking, looks at and addresses the singing bowl.

When it comes around again to the Wisdom Keeper, Sarah presents a brief précis of the topic for the circle. Prior to this Sunday she has called on the circle to focus on the issues of severely reduced school budgets and its impact on students. In an e-mail to each of the twelve chosen for this month's circle she sent some basic data and comments from the local papers. She suggests that, once again, students and teachers are becoming victimized and need to find creative ways to prevail.

For the next hour, one round of the circle after another, the twelve present their thoughts, their stories, their dreams and fantasies, their wisdom to the pot. As the circle shares, greater wisdom emerges and individually everyone in the room is led to think of new and creative roles for themselves to help their own kids and other kids to a richer and more fulfilling education.

At the end of the hour, the Wisdom Keeper asks the twelve for one final round in which to suggest possible themes for the next month's assembly.

Finally Sarah asks that each member reach out their hands toward the center and say their assembly prayer together.

May the abundance of the creation be present to us.

May the abundance of the creation give us strength to
live and power to prevail.

May the abundance of the creation enable us to be
peacemakers.

May the abundance of the creation guide us to enfeeble
domination and violence wherever we find it.

May all creatures come to the fulness of their role in the
cycle of life.

May the wisdom we have offered today be lifted up for
the life of the world.

May all people come and find themselves whole in our
fellowship with Jesus, the Galilean Sage.

Amen.

She moves to the center of the circle and strikes the singing bowl
again.

There is an unhurried, graceful bustle of activity as tables are moved,
chairs reset, silverware, napkins, and plates produced. The elders and
then the children take their turn filling their plates with the food that
has been carried to the assembly. Then the young people and adults
move to the buffet.

When most of the people are seated, Sarah once again strikes the
bowl, and there is silence.

Sarah: Lift up your hearts. (The people, a few picking up cue cards
from the tables, respond.)

All: We lift them up in praise.

Sarah: For the galaxies extend to eternity.

All: And their beauty is exquisite.

Sarah: Let us give thanks for the abundance of life on this earth.

All: Through it we and all people may be nourished.

Sarah: As we feast at this table of life.

All: May all the world come with us to the banquet.

(The singing bowl is lightly struck. The following is said by all in unison.)

All: We gather with reverence to the heart of love in all being. We celebrate the miracle of life nourished by the produce of the land.

(The singing bowl is lightly struck.)

All: We gather to remember our brother, Jesus.
         We remember how he sat and ate with his friends and enemies day after day.
         We remember how Jesus took bread, lifted it up, and said, "This is the bread of life given to sustain the people of the world."
         Let us share this bread and be strengthened to bring peace and justice to the world.

(The singing bowl is lightly struck.)

All: We remember how Jesus took a cup, lifted it up, and said, "This is the cup of life given to sustain the people of the world."
         Let us share this cup in solidarity with all the peoples of the world so that peace and justice may prevail everywhere.

(The singing bowl is lightly struck.)

All: Let us eat and drink and be glad. Amen.

There is a general outburst of happy conversation as everyone eats.

As the meal seems to come to its end, Sarah, as the Wisdom Keeper, has one more duty before relinquishing her role. The Wisdom Keeper and eleven others chosen to be in the circle for July must be drawn by lot. Although it is still three months away, the circle members need that much time to prepare for their responsibility. Sarah rings the singing bowl and asks for quiet so she can announce who is chosen. She reaches into the singing bowl, pulls out a chit and reads off the name that's written there. That person is the Wisdom Keeper for July. Then she reads the names of eleven more. The circle for July is now chosen by lot from among those over sixteen years of age who have come to three or more of the monthly assemblies. As the names are announced, all of the members make a silent promise to send their best energy to the people selected to discern the wisdom in July.

As her last act, Sarah delivers the list of all members and other necessary papers over to the Wisdom Keeper for May.

INTRODUCTION

The more piety in a given culture, the more likelihood of
pernicious systemic evil.

—*PRL*

After I wrote the checklist that appears on the back of this book and in the first pages, I set it aside and didn't look at it again until I had finished writing the core of the book. I see now that the checklist is a reflection of my present state of mind about the place of religion, and the Christian Church in particular, in the world today.

I have come to this condition as a result of a long career as a professional Christian, a priest of the Episcopal Church. I made a noble start to my career as a priest. I wanted to change the church; to make it a closer reflection of the values and life I saw in the person of Jesus. But the church changed me. First, as I attempted to learn its patterns and processes; how it worked. Next, as I worked within its structure. Then it changed me again as I confronted its deep systemic disease.[1]

---

[1]   The church, as I have known it, is undermined by two fundamental lies that create ongoing systemic dissimulation at every level and in every corner of its life. The first fundamental lie is that there is a God who intervenes in human affairs to deliberately wound some people while graciously and mysteriously rescuing others. The second is that the

I became disillusioned.

I spent a decade in recovery as an organizational consultant and political organizer. I went back into the professional ministry with a more radical stance to see if it was possible to build a congregation based on the wisdom tradition of Jesus and not so much on the old doctrinal traditions. My experience in the last twenty years tells me it is possible, but only with radical recision and reconstruction. Establishing new congregations is the easier path. And it is imperative that we recover and incarnate the power of Jesus' wisdom because we are at a major juncture in human history.

The crisis is now. The human race has an opportunity to capitalize on an oceanic increase in knowledge and understanding of the universe in which we live. At the same time we have achieved the capacity to obliterate life on the planet. Our deep desire for peace, plenitude, and delight, which I call abundance, is contradicted by our seemingly submissive captivity in a culture that is cascading into extreme violence and a massive exploitation of natural resources. We need today, perhaps more than ever, the deeply buried wisdom of the sages; wisdom that has been mostly submerged in a sea of pious aristocratic self-justification.

History does provide us with visions of a peaceable kingdom. The guidelines to it in our sacred Scriptures are, however, almost

---

soul of this God is a divine element in the human soul of Jesus. An elaborate cathedral of ritual, doctrine, and theology is erected on those foundations and paradoxically the edifice is structured to sustain the fictional footings under it. Disintegrity arises because there a very few individuals within the church who actually live as though the lie were the truth. They function day to day on the basis of a naturalistic, scientific world view, amiably suspending their disbelief in order to go along with a sacrosanct deceit.

totally unreliable because they reflect the values of a violent hierarchical society. I will say more about this in chapter 2. That does not mean to say that our traditions are barren of wisdom and empty of sound teaching. Trustworthy guidance is buried under the detritus of an aristocratic domination culture and needs to be ferreted out.

What was the wisdom in Jesus' teaching and program that so profoundly moved so many people in the first century c.e.? What was it that caused so many to tell tales about him, elevate him to honorific status, and write novels about him?

The written Gospels, and there are more than the four in our Bible, are the interpretive works of literate, and, therefore, probably upper-class men trying to fit the radical Jesus[2] into their own unique cultural frame. The Gospel writers came to the person of Jesus with their own set of myths and foundational sagas, some from Hellenic culture and some from the law and the prophets of Hebrew religion. They attempted to reconcile what they knew about Jesus with their own foundational stories and beliefs. So it was that "In the half-century before the creation of the first narrative gospel—the Gospel of Mark . . . [Jesus] a visionary sage was transformed from an iconoclast to an icon and his radical vision of God's domain dissipated in debates about divinity."[3]

In order to get realistic information about the compelling aspects of Jesus' vision and program we need to identify the influences that shaped the interpretive notions of those upper-class, literate Gospel

---

[2] The Jesus who is being rescued from ancient and outmoded doctrinal formulations by contemporary scholarship, particularly by the scholars of the Jesus Seminar; pioneers of the 3rd Quest for the Historical Jesus. See bibliography.

[3] From a flier promoting a recent Jesus Seminar on the Road sponsored by the Westar Institute.

writers. We need to discern, for example, how and why was it that the story about the death of Jesus was reframed to conform to the traditional sacrificial religion of the Temple in Jerusalem. Or, in another instance, how Jesus' life and death was viewed as the fulfillment of the Servant Songs in the book of the prophet Isaiah. When those interpretations are cleared away, we may be better able to perceive Jesus as he himself spoke and acted, knowing our vision will still be a bit blurry.

Then we must deal with the radical differences between the first-century agrarian culture of the Mediterranean world and our postindustrial culture of the twenty-first century. We are fortunate that sophisticated disciplines like archeology, sociology, and cultural anthropology have been applied to first-century Mediterranean culture. Now we can listen to and look at the specific things Jesus said and did in the context of his culture, not ours. It is possible for us to discern the impact his words and deeds had on the domination system that characterized the structures and meanings in the rural, agricultural, imperial culture of Roman-occupied Palestine.

Oppressed people who either met Jesus in person or heard his stories from others immortalized him. They built a number of local cults around him because his program liberated them from the oppressive economic and political forces that prevented them from experiencing abundant life. By his healing, his parables, his actions, he led people into a different way of thinking, being, and acting. Briefly put his imperatives were:

> Act as though my loving, merciful, bountiful Father
> was the emperor and not Caesar.
> Act as though you yourselves are high priests and reject
> the high priest in Jerusalem.
> Act as though the violence of the powerful is impotent
> and show them the power of love.

> Act as though money was dirt;[4]
> invite everyone to your tables and share whatever
> you have with one another.
> Act as citizens of the new Empire of God, which is now,
> is coming, and will be.

If we are to be liberated from the violence and excesses of our culture and experience the fulfillment of a universal dream of a peaceful, abundant life, we will have to do today what Jesus was doing in his day. Our enlightened state of mind says, contrary to all the religious extremists, that there is no God to rescue us, now or in any world to come. Jesus is not God's Messiah who will come at some surprising moment to make the world (or you) right. There won't be a solution to the human predicament unless it is our own. We must find power in ourselves to live out the vision of a New Human Being: To move into an era in which all peoples can live free of the domination system and the violence which enforces it; a new time in which social justice is understood as distributive rather than retributive or punitive justice (see glossary).

Following the example of those small local groups that were caught up in Jesus' vision and program, we need to form small communities that reincarnate Jesus' visionary program, circles of people living the power, and the practice that can lead the world to an age of abundance.

We will need to discover among ourselves the spiritual power of companionship with Jesus. In order to fulfill his vision, we will

---

4   If you read Jesus' line, "Then give to the emperor the things that are the emperor's, and to God the things that are God's," with a tone of utter contempt for Caesar, you get my point. "Give to the contemptible bastard emperor . . . etc." (Luke 20:25) Other scholars see Jesus retort as saying, "Have nothing to do with the impure coin and the impure empire of Caesar. Stick with the (just and benevolent) Empire of God." It may still have had a contemptuous tone.

need, like him, to sever ourselves from all the notions, assumptions, ideas, symbols, and rituals[5] that sustain our domination culture. We need to shrive ourselves of the givens of our culture that are embedded in our minds by our socialization as children and youths. To be a student and follower of Jesus today will compel us systematically and nonviolently to undermine the accepted structures, codes, and the religious validations of our culture and heal its victims.

We, human beings, make up words to identify and indicate relationships between phenomena "out there" beyond our sense apparatus. Some of that constructed, made-up "reality" is then sanctified and made in to incontrovertible "truth." Ernest Becker[6] alleges that all of the social construct of culture is an effort to avoid the fact of human mortality—the fear of our own death. The true meaning of redemption is, however, to recognize that the words and ideas which are said to be true are, in fact, fictional. Then it may be possible for us to live beyond our naive trust in the inherited truths; to live dying to yesterday, taking radical delight in today, in eager expectation of the very next moment of our newly created freedom to be New Human Beings

Contrast that notion with the blind assertion that the culture we have created is divinely sanctioned truth, validated by the Creator and God of all; that our foundational religious beliefs are "The Truth." Never is such havoc perpetrated as when the young are asked to fight and die for the "Truth" of our constructs. Never is such havoc perpetrated as when the young are asked to kill for the "Truth" of their own people. Liberation is to know that we can make up new words, new societies, new governments, new institutions, New Human Beings, and new relationships that transcend our anxieties and fears.

---

5   Like, for example, violent games and sports.

6   Becker, Earnest, *The Denial of Death,* (New York: Free Press, 1973).

I am suggesting that we initiate a process of transformation; of ourselves, our families, our small communities, and finally, our society. Working on self-transformation alone or one on one is nearly impossible. We need the support, encouragement, and companionship of others on the same transformative journey. I call it the Way of Jesus or The Way.

For the foreseeable future it is a small group process. Changing the pervasive domination culture will take generations, perhaps even more than the eighty or so since the death of Jesus. During our lifetimes we will continue to live in small assemblies of abundant generosity in the midst of a culture deprived of its potential richness by the fears which keep it in bondage to the domination system.

That means we will have to learn to live in two different dimensions of reality. Religious people have lived in two dimensions of reality for centuries. One traditional religious trick has been to posit a "spiritual" dimension in which one can develop an inner tranquillity as a retreat from the "material" dimension which is the sturm and drang of everyday life. The other trick has been to divide reality into this painful world of time and space, and another blissful world beyond death called heaven. Neither of those fake options will deceive us. The two dimensions we will live in as New Human Beings are both "material." They are social, economic, and political realities; one is the domination system and the other is our inbreaking world of abundant generosity.

It may not be easy. The very existence of a group of people who live abundantly while ignoring the truths and values of the dominant culture threatens that culture. Any overt action that calls into question the basic assumptions that the majority holds dear is a dangerous project. The elites of our day, as well as their stewards and their serfs, need desperately to hang on to the fictions—the truths and the constructs that allay their fears and, they believe, assure their everlasting well-being.

The long-term goal is the creation of a New Human Being. We have to start with the human being we are and become transformed.

This book sets out a way for a group to become self-transforming and to empower its members to become agents of healing, liberation, and abundance consistent with the values of the visionary sage, the historical Jesus. The phenomenon called the Resurrection means nothing unless there is an endless supply of people ready to embody Jesus—generation after generation seeking to move the world toward the fulfillment of Jesus' Domain of Divine Justice.

I am proposing a way of being together with other seekers that has great potential for transformation because it incarnates a new social structure: the circle.

This is what the rest of this book will cover.

Chapter 1 describes my own journey to the Jesus for today's world, how I learned about the power of circles and woke up to the domination system.

Chapter 2 unfolds the prevalence of the domination system in both the first and twenty-first centuries.

Chapter 3 describes the similarities and differences between Jesus' culture and ours so that we can better understand his mission and methods in his cultural context.

Chapter 4 looks at the Way of the itinerant visionary sage, Jesus, and its social impact on his own people and suggests how we might convert his work and teachings into a way in the twenty-first century that can help us to become New Human Beings—healed, liberated, committed to distributive justice and rejoicing in the potential of abundance of life for all.

Chapter 5 answers the question, "Why circles?" and shows how they work to fulfill our need for personal and social transformation that conforms to the Way of Jesus.

Chapter 6 describes the circle process in detail.

Chapter 7 shows how to design the circle process for large assemblies.

Chapter 8 presents some topics groups might use for getting deeper into the Way of Jesus.

As you read on, you will discover some idiosyncratic words and phrases that the glossary may help clarify. I am trying to weed the language of the domination system out of my thinking and writing. In chapter 7 I have, for example, used the word *syndic* where I might have used the word *representative*. I chose to do that because representative seems now to mean "advocate of our point of view against your point of view." Syndic has almost the same dictionary definition, but it is less familiar and can be infused with a noncompetitive sense.

CHAPTER 1

How I Got to Three Foundational Perceptions: Jesus, the Itinerant Visionary Sage, the Circle Process, and the Domination System

The stronger and more compelling a man's belief,
the greater danger he is to society.

—PRL

Robert Funk, one of the founders of the Jesus Seminar, claims that the original sin is self-deception. I plead guilty. I am also opinionated. Much as I try to free myself from cultural imprinting and view the world around me with new clarity of eye, heart, and mind, I know that is a vain task. My life experience has shaped me in a particular and unique way. Based on that way I reshape the world around me to fit my familiar patterns and conclusions—my fantasies about how things are. I know that I am limited. I badly need the wisdom of others to help me shape a richer and fuller vision of reality. Please keep these factors in mind as you read this book and argue with its contents.

In the beginning was Jesus.

I vividly remember sitting around a circular preschool-size table in the basement of the South Congregational Church in New Britain, Connecticut, singing what is probably the first song I ever learned.

> Jesus loves me. This I know,
> For the Bible tells me so.
> Little ones to him belong;
> They are weak, but he is strong.
>
> Yes, Jesus loves me.
> Yes, Jesus loves me.
> Yes, Jesus loves me.
> The Bible tells me so.

So I began my lifelong love affair with Jesus, the Galilean sage. In the bosom of my family, my parents, and grandparents, I learned about his love for me. The lesson continued in the South Church in New Britain. It was a remarkable church with an excellent Sunday school and youth program. In Sunday school I came to know intellectually and emotionally about the love of Jesus for me and for every kid in town. As a teenager in the Youth Group, under the tutelage of the Reverend Theodore S. Dunn, I learned about non-canonical Gospels. I remember one evening when we read aloud from one of them and heard some wild stories about Jesus as a boy. That's how we knew that there were more ancient stories about Jesus than there were in the New Testament. For me the heart of all of the stories about Jesus, all of the many Gospels, was Jesus' love. It was his love and generosity that moved me to honor and follow him.

I did not then and have never really believed that Jesus was "The Savior" whose death reconciled me to a God from whom I was alienated by my sinfulness. He was my ideal, my image of a human being perfected by love. And I knew that he loved me. I knew it from that song and the loving people who sang it with me. His love, it seemed to me, melded with the love and generosity of my family.

And there was too the love and generosity of friends and mentors. It was enough to make him the central figure and model for my life. Jesus is the first of all beings in my life. He is the person whose life is most worth emulating and growing into.

I confess what is obvious: My relationship with Jesus has not made me a better human being. I am wholly mired in limitation, in imperfection. I fall short. I don't think that is a problem or issue that limits this discussion, because unless you are a nonhuman alien, it is the same for you. We are all the same—imperfect human beings struggling to find ways to live in satisfying, harmonious, and graceful abundance.

For me, Jesus is a man, not God. He was neither divinely sired nor divinely chosen. He is not one part of a Holy Trinity. Reason tells me that the traditional God of monotheistic or, more accurately, tritheistic Western Christian religion does not exist and never has existed. I call myself, therefore, a nontheist follower of Jesus. As a nontheist, I throw out all the god-talk baggage of creedal, traditional, and fundamentalist Christendom. I revel in the person of Jesus revealed in his words and actions, unpolluted by the interpretive filters of Greco-Roman or Hebraic theism.

The person of Jesus revealed in his words and actions has been most clearly portrayed by the scholars of the Jesus Seminar. Through a laborious, collaborative process, the members of the seminar have settled on a very clear idea of what Jesus actually said and did. Robert Funk and the seminar scholars published their conclusions in a new Gospel, *The Gospel of Jesus.* It is widely available along with other books by the seminar scholars.[7]

For me, the most impressive of the seminar scholars is one of its founders, John Dominic Crossan, author of *Jesus: A Revolutionary*

---

[7]   See bibliography.

Biography and *The Essential Jesus: Original Sayings and Earliest Images* and several other truly significant books about the historical Jesus. I have read most of his books and many of his articles and have been privileged to come to know him personally. I tend to rely on him because he says most succinctly what I accept and affirm as foundational in Jesus' teaching and actions. In other more honest words, I agree with him because he agrees with me. His influence on me will be evident to all who know his work.

Over the last fifteen years, through my reading and study of the seminar scholars, I have come to see Jesus in the context of his culture; see him in a way that I had never seen him before. Wondrously, he is the same man I knew as a child. Now he is leading me to follow his program for a new humanity—a specific way, with not only the emotional aspects of my childish love, but strategies for healing and sociopolitical action. When I was a child, I saw as a child; now as an adult (thanks to the help of many), I see as an adult and see ever more clearly how and where to go along this way.

Today there is momentous urgency to find and follow new ways of being human. Around the world people are expressing a need for goals and strategies for the transformation of human beings and human society. During these first years of the twenty-first century, many are learning that there is no longer time and energy for theological or philosophical discussion about the ultimate nature of things. All life on this planet is endangered by greedy profiteering and stupidity in high places. My grandchildren and children everywhere are growing to adulthood threatened by the degradation of both the planet and civilization. Now is the time to struggle against the powers and principalities whose goals are short-term profits and the accumulation of personal wealth, and who no longer care for the earth or its inhabitants.

I am firmly convinced that the most powerful program to meet the challenges of our era is the imitation of the Way of Jesus—his wisdom and life, what he taught, and how he lived. If you truly want to know "what would Jesus do?" then follow me in exploring Jesus' Way. It combines personal and social transformation. It is a way to new, abundant and beautiful life in all of its dimensions.

Jesus' Way is characterized by the courage to question our culture's most cherished truisms, to undermine its oppressive institutions and accept rejection and ostracism by the hierarchy and those who collaborate with them. Jesus' Way is characterized by a self-emptying healing generosity especially towards the victims of oppression of every kind. Jesus' love is expressed by his fierce call for justice, his ridicule of pride and pomposity, his healing hands and his delight at sitting for supper with all the folks, particularly the outcasts. Learning to act as Jesus acted and thinking as Jesus thought will bring us to an abundant life. At the final edge of Jesus' Way is an ecstatic, erotic combination of deep tranquility and utter precariousness, of living over the precipice of today into tomorrow.

On how I discovered the power and wisdom of circles.

In the 1960s I became fascinated with Amerindian spirituality and culture, and for several years one of my major recreations was reading about and immersing myself in as much Native American culture as possible. There is a common tendency to reshape what we observe from other cultures and other times into notions that serve our self-interest. What I was learning about Native American culture and thought had the opposite effect on me. It forced me to question how I knew what I knew. I had an epistemological crisis and conversion. I was changed by what I read and what I observed.

Here I want to focus on one aspect of an Amerindian worldview that seems to be characteristic of all North American tribes: the circle. To put it simply, right angles, squares, and rectangles do not reflect the roundness, circularity, and cycles of the universe around us. Indians live in roundhouses, tepees, and hogans. Their sacred rites take place in sweat lodges and kivas. We live in rectangular houses.

Listen as Black Elk[8] tells about his life in captivity after he and his people have surrendered to the white men. "After the heyoka (sacred clown) ceremony, I came to live here where I am now between Wounded Knee Creek and Grass Creek. Others came too, and we made these little gray houses of logs that you see, and they are square. It is a bad way to live, for there can be no power in a square.

"You have noticed that everything an Indian does is in a circle,
and that is because the Power of the World always works in circles,
and everything tries to be round.
In the old days when we were a strong and happy people,
all our power came to us from the sacred hoop of the nation,
and so long as the hoop was unbroken, the people flourished.
The flowering tree was the living center of the hoop,
and the circle of the four quarters nourished it.
The east gave peace and light,
the south gave warmth, the west gave rain,
and the north with its cold and mighty wind gave strength and
endurance.
This knowledge came to us from the outer world with our religion.
Everything the Power of the World does is done in a circle.
The sky is round, and I have heard that the earth is round like a ball,
and so are all the stars.
The wind, in its greatest power, whirls.
Birds make their nests in circles, for theirs is the same
religion as ours.

---

[8]   *Black Elk Speaks: Being the Life Story of a Holy Man of the Oglala Souix*, as told through John G. Neihardt (Flaming Rainbow) by Nicholas Black Elk, Electronic Edition published by the University of Nebraska Press at http://www.blackelkspeaks.unl.edu/toc.htm. p. 150.

The sun comes forth and goes down again in a circle.
The moon does the same, and both are round.
Even the seasons form a great circle in their changing,
and always come back again to where they were.
The life of a man is a circle from childhood to childhood,
and so it is in everything where power moves.
Our tepees were round like the nests of birds,
and these were always set in a circle, the nation's hoop,
a nest of many nests,
where the Great Spirit meant for us to hatch our children."

As I read more and more it became clear that Amerindians believed that knowledge and wisdom was the product of the input of every member of the community. Each person comes from a unique place in life—unique talents, skills, insights, experiences—and each is at a different stage of maturity and growth. Each person or representative of a family or clan sits in a different place on the circle of life, bringing his or her own perspective to the circle. Each sees the object in the center of the circle in a unique way. For a rich introduction to the circle as it is understood by some Amerindians, read *Seven Arrows* by Hyemeyohsts Storm. He spells this wisdom out in a most intriguing way. The true nature of an object, he says, is only clear when every person's perspective is heard and honored. If a simple thing like a stone looks different from every point on the circle, how much more complex it is to get clarity on an idea!

Even more significant for me was reading about council circles. I vividly remember reading Gene Weltfish's account of the Pawnee Council Circle planning their winter buffalo hunt. The representatives of each of the families sat in the circle around a fire and each in turn, sunwise around the circle, spoke whatever was on his or her mind— a recollection, a fable, a dream, a vision, a feeling. Around and around the circle, the offerings were made as if to the fire in the center. After a time, the council circle ended, and the next day everyone in the village knew their task and did it. No argument had been presented;

no motions had been made and seconded; no votes taken. The planning had been done, the jobs assigned, and the preparations completed. It happened as the result of sharing the wisdom.

I began to experiment with circles. I asked groups of friends and colleagues to help me stage circle experiences. I gave them some guidance about what we were going to do. I placed a simple array of objects in the center of the circle. I asked each person sunwise (clockwise) around the circle to say whatever he or she wished about that array—dreams, fantasies, ideas, descriptions, whatever. Our objective was to understand the significance of the array. Time after time, we were moved by the spiritual dimension of the event, the beauty and wisdom that emerged.

In the sixties and seventies, part of my work was in the new field of organizational development consulting. I used the circle method to help work groups to discern the nature of their problems and issues in depth. Then we would set the cluster of issues in the center and go around and around until we discovered creative solutions and the resources to apply them. In team-building interventions, I asked team members to address team issues in the circle format. They found that their wisdom as a group became available in a more powerful way and that blocks to team effectiveness that had seemed insurmountable became much easier to overcome.

In my work in the church I encouraged and counseled groups to use the circle for Bible study. (See appendix 3) Almost without exception, they found that it opened new wisdom and spiritual depth to their discussions. In most discussion groups, there are two or three self-assured "leaders" who dominate a kind of dialogic discussion and several other people who remain silent for the most part. In the circle way balance is restored and all voices have equal weight and equal authority. When I encouraged the use of the circle way in women and men's support groups the same thing proved true. After a check-in round[9] (in which members report on their life since the last meeting), sharing support groups tended to focus their circle on personal issues or concerns that had emerged the opening round

By far the most compelling power of the circle way was our use of it for organizational decision making and conflict resolution. I was searching for a way out of the traditional kinds of organization that are based on a hierarchical, conflict-oriented model of domination systems. I wanted something other than the parliamentary procedures set out in *Robert's Rules of Order*. I persuaded the vestry of our church to use the circle to do such things as consider and adopt the budget, consider and adopt program goals and strategies, and elect officers. After stating the issue at hand, we would go round the circle sunwise until we reached a consensus. We agreed that the wisdom of the whole group would emerge if we trusted the process and offered to the center our best gifts, whether those were dreams, fantasies, ideas, or convictions. Always the consensus just seemed to emerge. We all knew it without there being a question like, "Have we reached a consensus?" The circle method may seem to take more time, but the result is that good decisions are made, everyone has an input, and no one is overridden or outvoted. When the process ends no one is nursing leftover bad feelings. Organizational conflict becomes a memory. And, most surprisingly, when we set a time to adjourn the meeting, we complete our business in the time allotted without feeling pressured

Although I was not aware of it at the time, many others began to experiment with the circles. Their experiments emerged from their work as therapists, educators, counselors, and personal-growth trainers. Some have introduced circles in school, nonprofit and business settings. They report outstanding success wherever they have applied the method. Their experience lends great validity to the power of circles to transform both people and their institutions.

---

[9]   More on check-in when we get to circle norms.

Christina Baldwin, one of the circle-way pioneers, has publFished what may be the primary book in the field.[10] She dramatically presents the centrality of circles in Amerindian and other premodern cultures.

Jean Shinoda Bolen, the well-known and widely read Jungian therapist, has written a poetic small book called *The Millionth Circle: How to Change Ourselves and the World* [11] in which she proposes, "nothing less than the visionary possibility that women's circles can accelerate humanity's shift to a post-patriarchal era." Except for the fact that she leaves men totally out of the process, it is a powerful little book.

The circle process has been used with great effectiveness by Alcoholics Anonymous groups for decades. The group leader announces a topic for the meeting, and the participants offer their insights, fears, hopes, and experiences in turn, around the circle, for the time allotted. The process evokes immense support for those struggling with addiction and codependency

Then a year ago I read Cecile Andrews's book, *Simplicity Circles,*[12] in which she writes an eloquent description of her experience with circles of folks across the nation who are seeking to learn how to live more simply. Cecile and her cohorts are experiencing the rebirth of a phenomenon which began more than a century ago.

---

[10] *Calling the Circle: The First and Future Culture.* See bibliography. Baldwin's sense of the future culture is, I think, compromised by her notion that hierarchical systems and peer systems like circles can complement one another in the same institutions. I think she vastly underrates the coercive power of domination system and the violence that sustains it.

[11] *The Millionth Circle: How to Change Ourselves and the World,* (Berkeley: Conari Press, 1999).

[12] *The Circle of Simplicity: Return to the Good Life.* See bibliography.

Cecile and others have pointed out that study and discussion circles are key feature of adult education programs in Denmark and Sweden. Their origin, however, was in America. Study circles were an adult education strategy developed by the Chautauqua movement in New York in the 1870s. In 1915, about seven hundred thousand people were participating in fifteen thousand study circles in the U.S. The circle-study method was carried to Sweden by union, co-op, and temperance organizers and by the fledgling Social Democratic Party. In Sweden, it was a way to educate people at all levels of society in the arts of democracy and was seen as an answer to their problems of poverty and illiteracy. Study circles flourished in Sweden while the movement died away in the U.S. Today, most Swedish study circles are funded (but not controlled) by the government with a per-participant subsidy. It is said that nearly three million Swedes participate in over three hundred thousand study circles annually. Swedish communities have convened study circles to work through major issues facing their towns, with study-circle participants turning into activists who then have a significant impact on the larger sociopolitical forces that effect their lives.

As we have seen, many in the USA are readopting study circles. There is a new awareness that the tremendous social and environmental problems we face press us to take new responsibility for the common good. There is also the growing realization that our monumental problems require that everyone must be involved in developing solutions.

One emerging model was developed in the small city of Lima, Ohio. In 1992, the mayor's office, Ohio State University, and a multiracial Clergy Task Force initiated grassroots study circles on race relations involving hundreds of people. These were so successful that participants created further waves of study circles involving businesses, neighborhood associations, and schools. The next year they organized a conference to which forty community leaders from around the Midwest came to learn how to create community-wide dialogues on race in their own cities. They triggered a movement that is growing nationwide.

And, finally, how I woke up to the domination system.

Over the years I have struggled with issues of leadership, motivation, and group dynamics in small to large systems. I tried to figure out what kept deeply committed, intelligent, and highly motivated people from making their systems work for the common good. There is, of course, the one underlying factor that I mentioned at the beginning of this chapter; self-delusion is universal. Another is that each of us is just a bit crazy and out of touch with reality. But more and more I have come to believe that the failures are not so much a result of personal failure but are caused by the underlying structure of human systems as we have known them.

It may have been that same conclusion that led Peter Drucker to say some fifty years ago that a major challenge for our time was to find an alternative to the hierarchical system of human organization—a system, he said, based on the Egyptian army of 6000 BCE. It is, not surprisingly, the same system adopted by Moses to organize the Israelites. This story from the Book of Exodus is one of the best ancient descriptions of the system.

> Moses' father-in-law, Jethro, said to him, "What you are doing is not good. You will surely wear yourself out, both you and these people with you. For the task is too heavy for you; you cannot do it alone. Now listen to me. I will give you counsel, and God be with you! You should represent the people before God, and you should bring their cases before God; teach them the statutes and instructions and make known to them the way they are to go and the things they are to do. You should also look for able men among all the people, men who fear God, are trustworthy, and hate dishonest gain; set such men over them as officers over thousands, hundreds, fifties and tens. Let them sit as judges for the people at all times; let them bring every important case to you, but decide every minor case themselves. So it will be easier

for you, and they will bear the burden with you. If you do this, and God so commands you, then you will be able to endure, and all these people will go to their home in peace." (Exodus 18:17-23)

So, in the first axial age began the cultural manifestation of the hierarchical conspiracy, which is our common heritage. It goes like this.

Leader: "I will set the rules. You will follow and obey the rules, and I will care for you, protect you, and bring you into a land flowing with milk and honey."

Followers: "Since we want security and that beneficent land, we will be loyal and obey you."

Leader: "We'll organize a pyramidal system of power, and I'll be at the top. You'll be someplace below me. I'll be in charge of where you are in the system and what benefits you get. Your role in my hierarchy of power and privilege will depend on two things: 1) how productive you are for me and, 2) how obedient you are to me."

The problem is that followers and leader alike are human beings with all the flaws thereof. The followers inevitably fall short. They fail to obey. And the leader inevitably finds it impossible to deliver on his promise to feed, house, and protect. Since the leader's foremost need is to preserve and enhance his power, he finds it convenient to undertake a policy of benign or malevolent neglect of the least powerful of his inferiors. Because there are such human characteristics as greed and avarice, the superior usually manages to take as much as he can from his subordinates while giving as little as possible. The inevitable result is that the rich get richer and the poor get poorer.

It is a conspiracy because both the superior and the subordinates choose to enter into the covenant. The power elites love it that way, and the subordinates never seem to learn from their misery. Again and again, through history, leaders and their followers recommit to one another.

The ultimate factor in the hierarchical system, with the emperor, chief, dictator, president at the top and the rest of us somewhere down the pyramid, is the power of violence. The powerful exercise culturally and, sometimes, divinely sanctioned violence to enforce their "rules." Those at the lowest levels of society play their part in the hierarchical conspiracy by enforcing cultural "norms" with vigilante violence, such as assassination, lynching, beating, and cross burning

Theologian and biblical scholar, Walter Wink, describes it this way.

> The domination system is characterized by unjust economic relations, oppressive political relations, biased race relations, patriarchal gender relations, hierarchical power relations and the use of violence to maintain them all. No matter what shape the dominating system of the moment might take [from the ancient Near Eastern states to the Ax Romania to feudal Europe to communist state capitalism to modern market capitalism], the basic structure has persisted now for at least five thousand years, since the rise of the great conquest states of Mesopotamia around 3000 b.c.e.[13]

I believe that Jesus Circles are a powerful way to move beyond the domination system to the Way of a New Human Being.

---

[13] Wink, Walter, *The Powers That Be: Theology for a New Millenium*, (New York: Galilee-Random House, 1999), p. 39.

CHAPTER 2

The Domination System Then and Now

This chapter and the next review and compare the sociopolitical and socioeconomic cultures of first-century Palestine and our twenty-first-century world in order to provide a better understanding of Jesus' life and the impact of his work. As the book progresses, we will see how a better understanding of the vision, message, and program of the historical Jesus is the foundation of the personal and social transformation that can occur through the circle process. In this chapter we look at the prevalence of the domination system in both the first and twenty-first centuries.

Jesus was born into and lived in a culture characterized by an oppressive domination system instituted by the Roman conquest and occupation of Palestine, managed under Roman authority, and administered by Jewish collaborators (or client rulers) such as the Herods and the Temple authorities. He grew up in rural Galilee under a complex domination system which merged traditional Jewish codes with the laws and demands of imperial Rome. His violent death was orchestrated by the Roman administration in Jerusalem charged with keeping the peace.

Two words describe the essence of this system—oppression and violence. Violence or the threat of violence was the means by which

Roman oppression was maintained. One of their favorite cruelties was crucifixion.

The utter profanity of Roman violence is documented in an article on crucifixion by Joseph Zias,[14] which is posted on the Internet at www.centuryone.org/zias.html. He writes:

> Crucifixion as a form of state terror was widespread across the Roman Empire, which included Europe, North Africa and Western Asia. It originated several centuries before the Common Era and continued into the fourth century CE when the practice was discontinued by Constantine, the emperor of Rome. While its origins are obscured in antiquity, it is clear that this form of capital punishment lasted for around 800 years and tens if not hundreds of thousands of individuals were subject to this cruel and humiliating death. Mass executions in which hundreds and thousands died—such as the well-known crucifixion of 6,000 followers of Spartacus as part of a victory celebration along the Appian Way in 71 BCE—appear in the literature.

While many people believe that crucifixion was reserved for criminals only as a result of Plutarch's passage that "each criminal condemned to death bears his cross on his back,"[15] the literature clearly shows that this class of individuals was not the only ones subjected to this

---

[14]   Copyright1998 Joseph Zias All rights reserved. Joe Zias was the curator of archaeology/anthropology for the Israel Antiquities Authority from 1972 to 1997. He is now retired. He is available for public lectures throughout the world. You may contact him directly or through the CenturyOne Foundation. JOSEPH ZIAS PO Box 37209, Jerusalem, Israel 91371 E-mail: zias@inter.net.il

[15]   Plutarch (46–120CE) Mor.554A/B.

ultimate fate. Alexander the Great had 2,000 survivors from the siege of Tyre crucified on the shores of the Mediterranean.[16] In addition, during the times of Caligula—37 to 41CE—Jews were tortured and crucified in the amphitheater to entertain the inhabitants of Alexandria. Women are seldom if ever mentioned specifically in the ancient sources aside from two passages in the Mishna, one in Tractate Mourning 2.11, which suggests that women may have been sacrificed as well. The second reference is found in Sanhedrin 6.5 in which Simeon B. Shetah had 70 or 80 sorceresses hung in the city of Ashkelon. However, as crucifixion was widely employed with slaves, one can assume that in the ancient world its use was thus not limited by gender but mainly by class.

Crucifixion amongst the Jews was rare, and except for a few instances, the subject was stoned to death first and then hung on a tree in accordance with the biblical passage in Deuteronomy 21:22-23: "When someone is convicted of a crime punishable by death and executed, and you hang him on a tree, his corpse must not remain all night upon the tree; you shall bury him that same day, for anyone hung on a tree is under God's curse."

There was one notable exception to this passage in which the victims were first killed via crucifixion rather than being hung on a tree after death. This was the case with the high priest, Alexander Janneus, in which 800 Pharisees were crucified in Jerusalem in 267 BCE before their wives and children. While [the 800 were] on the cross, according to Josephus[17] the women and children were then slaughtered

---

[16]   Curtius Rufus, Hist. Alex. 4.4.17.

[17]   Josephus, Antiquities 12.256.

The traditional Jewish domination system is thoroughly documented in the Bible. From Moses to David, Solomon and Josiah, the code, the structure, and the violence are spelled out in the literature we call the Old Testament (or Covenant; that is to say the deal God allegedly made with the people of Israel).

If you are familiar with the Old Testament you are well aware of the violent God of Abraham, Isaac, and Jacob. You may be familiar with the stories I have briefly paraphrased below. To read the entire stories, go to appendix 1.

> The violence of God is demonstrated early on, shortly after Moses descends from Sinai. Jahweh directs Moses to inform the people that if any creature goes up to or touches the edge of Sinai, they shall not live. They will be stoned or shot with arrows. Exodus 19:9 ff.

> Occupying the land that God has promised will not be difficult for his people. Although Moses knows he will not go into the Promised Land, he assures Israel that God will destroy the peoples who already occupy the land. Exodus 31:1 ff.

> The divine will for Israel is revealed when Samuel, on behalf of the Lord, directs Saul, the newly anointed king, to attack Amalek and kill every living creature. 1 Samuel 15:1 ff.

> The tradition of divinely sanctioned violence continues when King David tells his men to kill his enemies and hang their bodies beside the pool at Hebron. 2 Samuel 4:12 ff.

> A bountiful harvest of violence is climaxed when a wise woman of the city of Abel Beth-Maacah beheads a rebel

and throws his head over the city wall to troops bent on vengeance. 2 Samuel 20:14 ff.

Some Psalms are battle songs ensuring God's support for violence. Psalm 21:8 ff. for example.

If God's chosen people are unfaithful, Jeremiah reveals that God will have no compassion when he destroys them utterly. Jeremiah 13:8 ff

The pervasive and violent domination system of Judeo-Roman culture is repeatedly manifested in many stories in the New Testament. Typical of their colonial administration, the Romans appointed client kings and tetrarchs and allowed local Jewish elites who were obedient and loyal to Roman hegemony to continue their program of Temple taxes and increase their traditional oppressive governance.

Again, as a reminder, a few examples that you can skip over if you are already convinced. The full texts may be found in appendix 2.

Matthew 21:33 ff. is a parable about Jesus. I call it a parable about Jesus because the scholars of the Jesus Seminar have it as gray, meaning that it was probably not told by Jesus. As the scholars see it, it was allegorized and put in Jesus' mouth by the author of the Gospel as an attempt to validate Jesus as the heir of God.

In the parable a landowner plants a fenced vineyard with a winepress and a watchtower. He leaves the country. When harvest time comes he sends slaves to collect his share. His tenants beat one, kill another, and stone a third. Then he sends his son. The tenants kill him too. Matthew finishes the story with an implied threat that the landowner (that is, God) will kill the tenants who killed his Son (Jesus). Ouch!

Mark 15:12 ff. is another parable about Jesus. You know the story of the trial and crucifixion of Jesus. Here's the list of violent acts in Mark's account:

1. Jesus is flogged.
2. Jesus is fitted with a crown of thorns.
3. He is struck and spat upon.
4. Simon is forced to carry the cross.
5. They nail or tie him to the cross.
6. They crucify two bandits.

In Acts 7:54 ff. Luke tells the story of some vigilantes who were offended by Stephen's proclamation so they dragged him out of the city and stoned him to death.

Luke tells a colorful story about vigilantism and official violence in Acts 16:17 ff. A slave girl with a "spirit of divination" is a profit center for her owners. She follows Paul's party and annoys Paul so much that he exorcises her demon. The owners take offense at the loss of their little moneymaker, seize Paul and his friends, and haul them to the magistrates who order them to be flogged with rods. They are then thrown in prison and shackled.

In 2 Corinthians 11 Paul boasts about his ability to absorb violent treatment and abuse—imprisonments, countless floggings, sometimes near death, thirty-nine lashes five times, three beatings with rods and one stoning. It almost sounds as if he enjoyed it.

The author of 1 Peter urges slaves to endure pain and suffering from their masters in order to follow the example of Jesus "who suffered for you." No mistake here. This violence is divinely sanctioned.

Has anything changed in twenty centuries?

- Although we no longer tolerate slavery in the USA, we systematically exploit illegal immigrants and Third World factory workers. We easily overlook slavery in other countries.
- We have sanitized (or is it humanized?) our mode of capital punishment. We use lethal injection and the electric chair instead of stoning and crucifixion.

- Although angry mobs have not recently lynched or assassinated Blacks, homosexuals are regularly beaten and killed by vigilantes.
- Although we like to call our police peace or public safety officers, our laws are enforced by the use of their power and violence (including sporadic vigilante-type beatings).
- Although we pretend to be a classless society, those regarded as being lowest on the scale of human value, Blacks and Chicanos, are arrested, jailed, and executed more frequently than the more influential, highly regarded affluent and white folks.
- Although we elect ordinary citizens to public office, once they are sworn in we magically attribute them with superior knowledge and authority.
- Corporations are perhaps the major manifestation of the domination system in our culture and most of them treat human beings as objects (means of production) whose services are at the will of and are considered as the right of the management elites. (In the late nineteenth and twentieth centuries the Labor Union Movement made major strides in obtaining rights for workers which protected them from arbitrary managements. In the last three decades, however, we have watched many of those rights erode and witnessed a great increase in the power of corporate management to abuse members of the workforce.)
- Our near addiction to violence in sports (notably professional wrestling, boxing, hockey, and football), movies, television, and video games is even more evidence of our cultural captivity in the domination system.

So not much has changed.

Our culture, with respect to violence and the domination system, is very congruent with the Roman Empire of the first century. We, like the people of the Holy Land in the first century, live in a domination system. We grow up in it. We accept violence and the domination system as a way of life without question. Our federal government and its budget are consumed with military power. Some say that the USA is the most militarized nation in history.

Because of our familiarity with life in a domination system we easily assume that our culture is the same as the culture of the Mediterranean world in the first century. We believe that we can simply pick up the Gospels and understand who Jesus was, what he said, and what he did. Though it is partly unconscious, this assumption leads even well-trained biblical scholars to misinterpret the material they study.

As citizens of a post-enlightenment culture, however, we have almost nothing in common with our first-century Mediterranean forebears. In order to understand Jesus for who he was in his own time and culture, we have to look at some of the major differences between our culture and his. When we set what Jesus did and said in the context of his own culture, we can better appreciate his impact on the dominant institutions that kept his people subjugated and got him killed by the Romans.

The quotation from Walter Wink at the end of the last chapter seems to assume that first-century Palestinian culture was much like our own. We operate within four interdependent domains: politics, economics, kinship, and religion—distinct clusters of institutions in which we live, by which we are socialized, and through which we realize the meanings of our lives. The social structure of the Mediterranean culture of the first century was, however, vastly different. In the next chapter we will attempt to understand the significance of those major differences. Then seeing Jesus in his own cultural frame, we may be better able to translate his message and program into our own culture

CHAPTER 3

The Once Rural Agrarian and the Now Urban, Postindustrial Culture

The issue isn't the meaning of life—that will forever remain
a culturally shaped conundrum,
which extends to encompass the known limits of the
universe.
What is an issue for all but the most leisured of human
beings is the question:
How do my people and I live an abundant, gracious, and
wholesome life
during our very brief part in the mysterious cosmic process?

We, human beings, tell ourselves stories and develop concepts that explain the universe in which we live. In the stories and concepts we learn the rules and strategies that enable us to live together in as close to well-being as possible. Our natural assumption is that we all, no matter what place or time we may occupy in history, tell the same stories. Once we have thought about it, we realize that we don't all have the same stories; but that the stories come from a specific time and place. The stories that were told in the villages of Palestine in the first century CE are different from the stories that are told in a modern high-rise in Chicago.

Again, our tendency is to read the ancient stories as though they are taking place in familiar territory. We read a story that Jesus told about a father and his sons, popularly known as the Parable of the Prodigal Son. Until we know better, the setting, the clothing, the background of the story are the ones we live in; maybe it's like the farming culture of contemporary rural Iowa transported to the rural Middle East. Our underlying assumptions about the relationships in agrarian first-century families, how they work and what values they hold, are the same as for our families today.

To our good fortune, we have developed methods of analysis in cultural studies, sociology, anthropology, archeology, statistics, and computer technology that enable us to know much of the intimate detail of life in the ancient world. Some have said that we know more about their society than the ancients themselves did. In general, what we have learned is that a rural, agrarian culture is vastly different than our urban, industrialized culture.

In this chapter I want to take advantage of what we have learned and outline the major areas of difference between the rural, agrarian, Mediterranean culture of first century in which Jesus lived, worked, and died and the urban, industrial culture in which we live. My objective is to help you to better understand the radical assault that Jesus made on the assumptions that were the social glue of his time and his society.

There are four main areas of difference between his culture and ours.

1. The social structure of the first century was less complex than ours.
2. Their understanding of personhood was vastly different.
3. The means of production and, therefore, the economic foundation of culture was different.
4. The social-class system was unlike ours.

This chart may help you visualize these areas of cultural difference.

	First Century	Twenty-first Century
1. Social Structure	Two Domains: Kinship and Polity	Four Domains: Domestic Life, Polity, Economy & Religion
2. Personhood	Collectivism	Individualism
3. Production	Agrarian/Rural	Industrial/Urban
4. Class Structure	Fixed	Fluid

In the succeeding pages I will attempt to unpack and explain the significance of the differences in each of the four areas.

1. Social structure: Two domains—Four domains

We need to take a brief look at the two domains of life in the first century. Some aspects of this two-domain social system will become clearer in the discussions about personhood, production, and class structure a bit further along.

Kinship: The family was the fundamental unit of life. The family heritage and tradition passed down through the male side of the family placed the extended family in its community, its rank in the class order, established and maintained its honor, and gave identity to its members. In agrarian societies the extended family was a unit of production. This was true for the poorest of the poor and the richest of the rich. Each was locked into a patrilineal system from which there was no escape. Women were embedded in one male or another, either father or husband or uncle. If not, they were nonpersons, castoffs with no honor and no purity. The eldest male, head of the extended household, presided over the family's religious practices. He was also responsible for paying the Temple and other taxes and, as such, was the broker between the family religion and the religion of the polis, the Temple.

Polity: As I use it here the term *polity* simply refers to the city-oriented processes of public order or governance. We know that the ultimate power was wielded by the Romans with the collaboration of client rulers, like the Herods and Temple officials. Wealthy landowners had their primary residences on their land in the countryside. They maintained secondary residences in the city where they gathered to joust for honor, preside over the flow of goods and services (the political economy), and participate in the religious (religious economy) functions of the Temple. While the Temple authorities maintained a regular round of ritual activities and celebrations for religious purposes, they imposed and collected Temple taxes. They were also the principal officers of a kind of bank. The Temple at Jerusalem was a depository in which the elites protected their cash surpluses from bandits and brigands.

Where did the elites get their money? The peasants and slaves worked the land. They produced a surplus; meaning they produced more crops than the landowners allowed them to keep for their survival. The landlord took the surplus and kept as much as he could after paying taxes to his patrons on up the line all the way to the emperor in Rome. Religion at every level supported and gave divine sanction to the system.

A profound implication for our understanding of Jesus' message and program is that everything he said or did impacted the whole of his culture. When he attacked the system of purity by healing lepers and the blind, it shook people at every level of the society. Both the Gospels of Mark and Matthew report that Jesus overturned the moneychangers' tables in the Temple at Jerusalem. While there is some debate among scholars about what actually happened in the Temple, the reports of it are a symbolic, if not actual, subversion of the economic/political/religious functions of the Temple in the Roman domination system. And it was, as well, a symbolic sabotage of the family of priests who ran the Temple and lived off of its taxes.

We tend to take it for granted that the four domains of our culture are a universal phenomenon, but they are a modern development; a product of the enlightenment and the industrial revolution. It was in the early years of the seventeenth century that the market and economics became identified as a domain in its own right. At about the same time the church and religion began to be separated from the civil state into its own domain. The industrial revolution and the democratic ideal gave rise to free entrepreneurship and class mobility.

Imagine what would happen today if Jesus walked into the Roman Catholic Cathedral in Boston and began to knock holy statues off their pedestals and called the prelates a nest of vipers and degenerates. The only political involvement would be that the police might be called to take him into custody and the municipal court sentence him to a term in prison, but it would have no effect on the economic health of Boston, and no effect on the domestic lives of any parishioners (except, perhaps, those who had been abused by priests over the years). In the minds of almost everyone aware of the incident, it would simply be the story of a religious nut working out his psychological or maybe theological or spiritual issues with the church.

Our social structure would be totally mystifying to Palestinians of the first century, and we would find the culture of Palestine in the first century as quaint to us as Bantu culture was to the first Europeans who encountered it.

The two diagrams below are an attempt to graphically portray the differences between our culture and theirs.

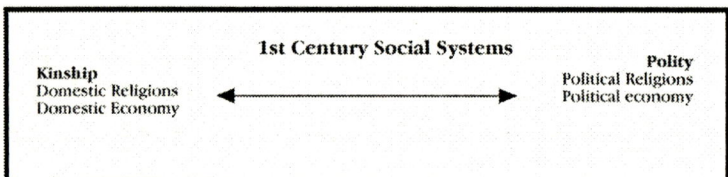

1st Century Social Systems

Kinship		Polity
Domestic Religions	◄─────────────────►	Political Religions
Domestic Economy		Political economy

```
21st Century Social Systems

Governance/Politics                                    Economy
Federal, State, Local                                  "The Market",
                          ◄─────────────►              Industry, Corporations

              ▲        ╲           ╱        ▲
              │          ╲       ╱          │
              │            ╲   ╱            │
              │            ╱   ╲            │
              │          ╱       ╲          │
              ▼        ╱           ╲        ▼

Domestic Life, Kinship,                                Religion
family life               ◄─────────────►              Including secular religions
```

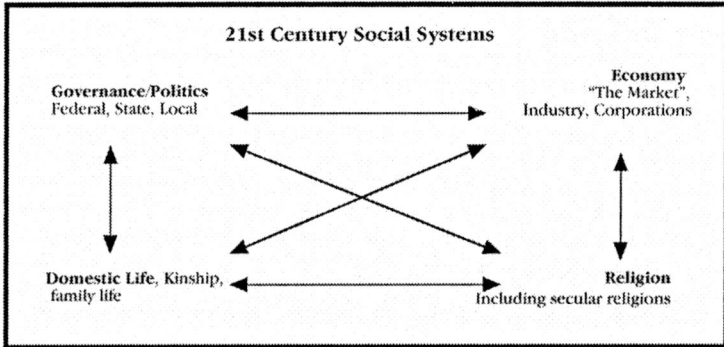

If we think about life as a process of juggling different sets of needs, demands, constraints, and opportunities, the people in an ancient, rural agrarian faced a more simple challenge than we do. They had only two domains to keep in the air. Domestic needs and constraints were either in harmony or conflict with the demands of political life. We are always juggling four domains. Virtually every issue in one domain has implications for and impacts the other three domains.

In the USA we are juggling with these issues which would be completely incomprehensible to a first-century Palestinian:

- The separation of state and religion is set in the U.S. Constitution. We are now debating the nature of the separation as a result of the push the religious right is making for "faith-based social programs" and "school vouchers." The issue has implications for each of the four domains— for families, for the economy, and for religious institutions. In the first century, religion was inhered in every aspect of life. Caesar was, after all, a God.
- Led again by the religious right, many in our culture campaign for programs to "strengthen family life." Yet those who advocate for stronger families seem unwilling to support government-financed social programs that might help poor families. The overall health of the economy as

well as tax policy and government subsidies have a major impact on the well being of families. We now are aware that in the South, "strengthening family life" is a euphemism for racial segregation. In first-century agrarian culture, discussions about a program to strengthen family life would be impossible.

- We debate governmental methods of controlling or at least modifying the economy. Free-market advocates, on the one hand, want minimal or no government regulation of the market. On the other end of the spectrum, socialists want no part of a free-market system. In the Palestine of Jesus' day the emperor was the economy.

- We debate the relative virtues of welfare. Some want government welfare subsidies to be severely limited or eliminated. Others believe welfare benefits should be strategically generous. In Mediterranean culture of the first century, a Judean head of household was responsible for seeing that everyone in his extended family was fed and that a corner of his fields were left unharvested for the benefit of the nonpersons who lived outside of kinship structures. And he had to accomplish this when most of his production was confiscated by the elites.

- Our society is in the midst of a debate about sexuality that has ramifications in all four domains of contemporary culture— for governance at every level, for domestic life, religion, and the economy. Shall the state declare homosexual marriage illegal or sanction it and give it the same protections and privileges as heterosexual marriage? And what role shall the churches play? This ongoing debate would be completely unintelligible to a first-century citizen.

2. Personhood: Collectivism—Individualism

The diagram (above) of the social system of the first century does not accurately represent the significance of kinship. A human being was identified by family relationships, and in a real sense one could not exist (be) outside of the family. In our postindustrial culture, accomplishment is the major factor in judging personal worth. My family history, my family connections, my extended family are really of little interest in measuring my social value, my self-worth, my significance and meaning as a person (that is, unless I, as an individual, choose to make it so). In the Mediterranean world of the first century it was exactly the opposite. What defined a person was the family's worth and honor, meaning and being, significance and status. It was the same in the cultural domain of public life, of governance and dominance in the cities as it was among peasant farmers and villagers.

In reading the New Testament, therefore, it is critical that we not bring to it our post-enlightenment understanding of personhood. In thinking, for example, about parables or stories that touch on kinship, we might severely underestimate the significance of a break in the family. From our place in the twenty-first century, we might see the prodigal son as a young man following the advice of Horace Greely and going off into the West to make his own fortune.

From the perspective of first-century Mediterranean culture, however, he is a fool who is humiliating his father, bringing shame and dishonor to both his father and elder brother by leaving the family. The fact that the father was affluent enough to leave an inheritance is evidence that he is an elite, a wealthy landowner. The story also makes the father a fool, dishonoring himself by giving the younger son his inheritance when he asked for it.

In leaving his family, the younger son has ventured into non-personhood. Those listening to the story would ask, "Why would anybody do that?" His family is shamed and dishonored by his action. Then the young man doesn't find new kin. He finds a "family" with pigs; he eats with (impure) pigs, further shaming himself. In the eyes of the listeners, he has been totally degraded.

By our individualistic standards he has had terrible luck and maybe made some stupid decisions. In any case, we would simply say that he has failed to make it on his own. The son decides to return home. In the first century, however, the shame the younger son will bring back to his family is not about personal failure, but about having become a totally shamed nonperson.

He brings that shame home. In so doing he increases the dishonor and shame to his family. Amazingly, he is welcomed back with a feast, gifts, and a fatted calf. The listeners ask, "What's going on here?" In this story Jesus is saying once again, "We invite the pure and impure, the landowner and the peasant, the shamed and dishonored to feast together in the new domain of God."

In the framework of his culture Jesus (or the narrator of the story in the Gospel)[18] is telling a tragicomic, soap-opera-type story that ridicules whole notion of shame and honor. He nonviolently overturns this imprisoning and oppressive patriarchal aspect of the domination system.

I wonder if Jesus' greatest offense to the Judeo-Roman elites of Sepphoris, Tiberias, and Jerusalem was his disdain for and ridicule of the whole construct of shame and honor that structured their society. If this is true his repeated invitations to an open-table feast were powerful political acts.

3. Production: Agrarian/Rural to Industrial/Urban

Jesus lived in an agrarian/rural society. In spite of the presence of cities, the great centers of culture, government, trade, religion, and learning like Rome, Alexandria, Jerusalem, and Istanbul, the relative well-being of nearly everyone was dependent upon the land and its productivity. Landholding was the source of wealth for the elites on

---

[18]   The Jesus Seminar has this parable in Luke 15 as pink.

whose patronage depended the lives of those who tilled the land. The elites built second homes in the cities or in the case of Sepphoris (some four miles from Nazareth) and Tiberias, built new cities in which to display the wealth and the honor they extracted from their landholdings. It is a mistake to assume the elites were urban folk. They were identified with their landholdings. Their city homes were secondary places of relaxation, socializing, and display.

Their town homes were second homes. Their city life was analogous to the second homes in the mountains owned by the elites of modern cities.

I need to say more about elites. I use this term to identify the upper crust of society. The elites were extended families (or kinship groups) who, through inherited power and wealth, were able to control and expand their landholdings with the help of their retainers. The elites made up about 5 percent to 6 percent of the population. Those called retainers (again members of kinship groups) were their police, their stewards, their armies; in other words, those responsible for keeping order and keeping the wealth of the elites growing and safe. The labor of about 95 percent of the population was necessary to support the elite 5 percent.

We live in an urban, industrialized society. Almost every aspect of our daily life is governed by principles and processes developed during the eighteenth-century industrial revolution. From then onward the industrial revolution proceeded in a series of incremental steps, the most recent of which began with the development of computers and the silicon chip.

During the first phase of the industrial revolution, typical crafts, such as weaving and metalwork, moved from the homes and small shops of craftsmen to large factories near sources of water power. In the late eighteenth century in America, Eli Whitney initiated the second stage when he introduced the concept of standardized parts for rifles produced for the American Revolution. Then water power was augmented by—and eventually overcome by—steam power, and in the late nineteenth century, Col. Hard D. Weed, inventor of the Weed Tire Chain, electrified the first factory, a bicycle shop in upstate New York. That innovation freed factories from riversides and millponds and led eventually to the next phase, which appeared at the turn of the twentieth century.

The next phase of industrial development is attributed to Henry Ford who developed the assembly line. He saw that it was more efficient to move products through a line of part depots than to bring parts to one place of assembly.

The shift from a rural, agrarian society to urban, industrial society entered another stage with the emergence of factory towns like my hometown, New Britain, Connecticut, and cities like South Bend and Gary, Indiana and Detroit, Michigan. The increasing use of steam and gasoline engines to power agricultural equipment (associated with names like John Deeree and Cyrus McCormick) made the industrialization of all human activity seem possible and have great potential for the well-being of people everywhere.

In the late twentieth century, with the development of computer-driven machines, the process becomes even more efficient and less labor intensive. That phenomenon, coupled with the increased use of highway transport, has liberated the factory from the city and moved it out to suburban and exurban industrial malls.

The latest phase, computerization, with which all of us are familiar, some call the second industrial revolution because of the radical, incremental increase in processing information, automating manufactures, and speeding distribution. Others say we now live in a postindustrial society; the information age.

Now, in the twenty-first century, the potential exists for the labor of 5 percent of the population to free 95 percent from productive work. Though that potential may exist, there is no sign that the benefits of wealth, health, and well-being are even trickling down to the masses of people at the bottom of the economic pyramid. In 1997 the wealthiest 1 percent of families in the USA owned roughly 39 percent of total net wealth, the top 10 percent of families owned over 72 percent, and the bottom 40 percent of the population owned less than 1 percent.

4. Class structure: Fixed—Fluid

Jesus and his friends lived in a society characterized by the profound influence of kinship bonds. At whatever level of the society, family connections shaped the entire life course of every person. Being born into a family of wealth and power meant that wealth and power would be your heritage. This is probably most familiar to traditional Christians and Jews who have long read about the Aaronic priesthood, those who by birth were Temple priests.

> The LORD spoke to Moses: Then you shall bring Aaron and his sons to the entrance of the Tent of Meeting, and shall wash them with water, and put on Aaron the sacred vestments, and you shall anoint him and consecrate him, so that he may serve me as priest. You shall bring his sons also and put tunics on them, and anoint them, as you anointed their father that they may serve me as priests, and their anointing shall admit them to a perpetual priesthood throughout all generations to come. Exodus 40: 12-15

The well-being (read: wealth) of the Aaronic family was assured by the allocation of lands given them as described in Joshua 21.

> Then the heads of the families of the Levites came to the priest, Eleazar, and to Joshua, son of Nun, and to the heads of the families of the tribes of the Israelites; they said to them at Shiloh in the land of Canaan, "The LORD commanded through Moses that we be given towns to

live in, along with their pasture lands for our livestock." So by command of the LORD the Israelites gave to the Levites the following towns and pasture lands out of their inheritance.

The lot came out for the families of the Kohathites. So those Levites who were descendants of Aaron, the priest, received by lot thirteen towns from the tribes of Judah, Simeon, and Benjamin.

These towns and their pasture lands the Israelites gave by lot to the Levites, as the LORD had commanded through Moses.

Out of the tribe of Judah and the tribe of Simeon they gave the following towns mentioned by name, which went to the descendants of Aaron, one of the families of the Kohathites who belonged to the Levites, since the lot fell to them first. They gave them Kiriath-arba (Arba being the father of Anak), that is Hebron, in the hill country of Judah, along with the pasture lands around it. But the fields of the town and its villages had been given to Caleb, son of Jephunneh, as his holding.

To the descendants of Aaron, the priest, they gave Hebron, the city of refuge for the slayer, with its pasture lands, Libnah with its pasture lands, Jattir with its pasture lands, Eshtemoa with its pasture lands, Holon with its pasture lands, Debir with its pasture lands, Ain with its pasture lands, Juttah with its pasture lands, and Beth-shemesh with its pasture lands—nine towns out of these two tribes. Out of the tribe of Benjamin: Gibeon with its pasture lands, Geba with its pasture lands, Anathoth with its pasture lands, and Almon with its pasture lands—four towns. The towns of the descendants of

Aaron—the priests—were thirteen in all, with their pasture lands. Joshua 21:1-4, 8-19.

This illustrates the process by which the elites obtained the power and wealth that passed from one generation to the next and the centrality of the priesthood and the Temple at Jerusalem to the economy of aggrandizement. It also indicates the divine sanctions, which sustained their continued dominance. With the Roman occupation of Palestine the situation of the dominant elites changed. While the Romans were content to let the traditional families continue to govern the society (under their oversight) they exacted taxes and liens, which forced an even deeper shift from wealth as landholding to wealth as agricultural surpluses. The demand for production caused the landowners to drive small farmers into bankruptcy, accumulate larger landholdings, and force dispossessed farm families into poverty.[19]

Governance meant exercising power over the laborers, merchants, and craftsmen. As it is in every dominance system, the power of the elites was exercised by their retainers—soldiers, police, stewards. These represented another kinship group, and their work was passed from one generation to another. It may have been possible for some to make a shift from a lower to an upper class, but that was, in the view of most scholars, a rarity.

1 Kings 9:15 ff. (How Solomon got his slaves and made Israelites his retainers.)

This is the account of the forced labor that King Solomon conscripted to build the house of the LORD

---

[19]　The process was not unlike that which drove many small Irish farmers off their land. In the USA a similar process has occurred as gigantic agricultural corporations take over the land of small family farmers.

and his own house, the Millo, and the wall of Jerusalem, Hazor, Megiddo, Gezer, Lower Beth-horon, Baalath, Tamar in the wilderness, within the land, as well as all of Solomon's storage cities, the cities for his chariots, the cities for his cavalry, and whatever Solomon desired to build, in Jerusalem, in Lebanon, and in all the land of his dominion. All the people who were left of the Amorites, the Hittites, the Perizzites, the Hivites, and the Jebusites, who were not of the people of Israel—their descendants who were still left in the land, whom the Israelites were unable to destroy completely—these Solomon conscripted for slave labor, and so they are to this day. But of the Israelites Solomon made no slaves; they were the soldiers, they were his officials, his commanders, his captains, and the commanders of his chariotry and cavalry. These were the chief officers who were over Solomon's work: five hundred fifty, who had charge of the people who carried on the work.

According to this account, Solomon and his family, the elites, had the Israelites as his retainers and the people of the occupied territories as his slaves. This is a good, albeit simple, account of the realities that prevailed into the first century in Palestine.

The social-class structure was really a bit more complicated.[20]

The work of Gerhard Lenski is foundational in the analysis of class structure in agrarian cultures. He developed the figure below

---

[20] This discussion is based on the model of Gerhard E. Lenski from Power and Privilege: A Theory of Social Stratification (New York: McGraw-Hill, 1966), pp. 215–290 and the summary by John Dominic Crossan in The Historical Jesus: The Life of a Mediterranean Jewish

which captures the most basic facts about stratification in agricultural societies. The horizontal dimension represents the proportion of people at each level while the vertical dimension represents position in the stratification system. In agrarian societies farmers, peasants, and artisans may make up 90 percent to 95 percent of the population.

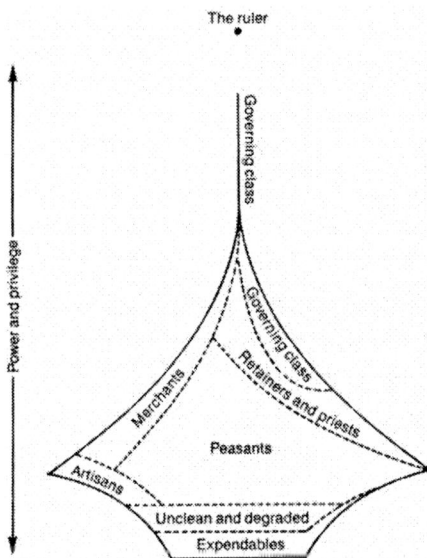

The Aristocratic or Upper Class:

1. The Ruler—Caesar was the one, the ultimate elite figure in the world, and it is no accident that he was godly enough to be a God. All of the wealth of his empire was his by right, and all others were subservient to him. Although there were numerous client kings in the East who held their positions

---

Peasant, (San Francisco: HarperCollins, 1991), pp. 45-46. The diagram is from Power and Privilege: A Theory of Social Stratification by Gerhard Emmanuel Lenski, Jr. Copyright © 1984 by the University of North Carolina Press. Used by permission of the publisher.

through imperial patronage, they were not rulers but prominent members of the governing class. The emperor directly received perhaps 25 percent of the empire's total income.

2. The Governing Class (about 1 percent of population)—received at least 25 percent of annual national income. These elites served as civic as well as military officers and advisors under the ruler; most of them as appointees of the ruler. They tended vast grants of territory and its peoples. They confiscated the wealth of the land and commerce to support their elite lifestyle and facilitated their civic responsibilities.

3. The Retainer Class (about 5 percent of population)—a small army of officials, professional soldiers, household servants, and personal retainers including scribes, bureaucrats, all united in service to the governing class and thence the emperor. They were the peacekeepers (police) and bureaucrats who were responsible for protecting and enhancing the elites' well-being.

4. The Merchant Class—carried on a modest amount of trade and commerce although the culture was agrarian and wealth came from land and farming. Some merchants who dealt with luxury goods could be quite wealthy, but most were poor. The wealthy tradesmen were not despised, because the elites used them to increase their own wealth. Small merchants were held in contempt.

5. The Priestly Class—in the Greco-Roman world the famous temples and shrines, frequently in important cities, were the focus of political religion. The priestly class performed the religious rituals and oversaw the Temple business. Their bounteous lifestyle was supported by the taxes which they exacted from peasants and other elites alike. Temple buildings were often richly adorned and served as repositories of wealth.

> Between the upper class and the lower class was
> a great gulf which no one bridged.[21]

The Plebeian Class or Lower Class:

1. The Peasant Class (vast majority of population) was the subsistence farmers and small landholders who worked the land and produced the agricultural surplus. They may have been able to retain about one-third of the crop they produced, while paying two-thirds or more in taxes. Since the elites were focused on increasing their wealth as a matter of honor, farmers were being more and more economically oppressed and small landowners forced off the land by foreclosure on their loans.

2. The Artisan Class (about 5 percent of population) was ranked below peasants. Because they had neither land nor status nor means of making advantageous marriages. As in most agrarian societies, artisans were recruited from the ranks of the landless peasants, either dispossessed or non-inheriting ones. Their ranks were continually replenished from migrants from the countryside.

3. The Unclean/Degraded Classes were those with occupations such as porters, miners, lepers, or were women with "issues of blood", or prostitutes, or those who dealt in "impure' things like the dead.

4. The Expendable Class (averaged 5 percent to 10 percent of the population, in normal times) included those forced to live by charity or by their wits, e.g., petty criminals and outlaws, beggars, and underemployed itinerant workers. At the very bottom of the social scale were the untouchables, scavengers, and beggars, who lived just outside the city.

---

[21] In general, the great divide in the Greco-Roman world was between those who had to work with their hands and those who did not.

Whatever kinship group you were born into remained your kinship group for life unless some terrible mishap brought you to a lower status. It was not uncommon for a small-landed farmer to be displaced by indebtedness and become a bandit, an expendable. Widows of artisans might become prostitutes, and sons of rich landowners might find themselves in a far land eating with unclean pigs.

One nicety of the domination system with its rigid social stratification was the relationship of patron of the upper class and his clients of the lower class. Ideally the patron was supposed to care for and protect his clients, peasants and artisans, and provide them with a sufficient livelihood. And the client was allowed in extraordinary circumstances to supplicate the patron for special help and favors. This byplay of patron and clients persisted into the enlightenment in aristocratic English households. The PBS series *Upstairs Downstairs* is a classic representation of the phenomenon. Both good and bad patrons and clients populate the series and class rigidity is at its core.

In twenty-first-century America it is possible for a near "expendable" to become an elite through music, professional sports, higher education, entrepreneurship and/or extreme good fortune. Racial, ethnic, and gender discrimination are the only impediments to moving up the social ladder, and they seem to be diminishing, albeit slowly. The slippery slope down to the bottom of the social ladder, however, is greased by our insistence on making alcohol and legal drugs easily available (and very attractive through their manufacturers' advertising campaigns). It is also greased by our equal, if not stronger, persistence on the absolute prohibition of nonprescription psychotropic drugs.

A question without an answer: What portion of the population in the first century was mentally ill? I raise that question because we now know that being homeless and living on the streets can make you crazy. Mental illness can be caused by social dislocation, oppression, and overbearing stress—the effects of the domination system. It is entirely possible that Jesus healed people made mad by poverty and homelessness by giving them a profound sense of their self-worth in the eyes of God.

What we have in common with Jesus is our lives in a domination system. In other respects the culture in which Jesus lived is not at all like the culture in which we live.

What did Jesus do to impact his people so powerfully in his time? If we answer that, we may be able to discern what he, or we, might be doing to impact our people in our time. Because Jesus was a threat to the elites of Galilee and Judea, the Roman retainers in Jerusalem decided to take him out. What was the nature of his threat and how is it that a lower-class illiterate[22] caused the elites so much anguish?

I will try to answer that question in the next chapter.

---

[22]   "If Jesus was a carpenter, therefore, he belonged to the Artisan class, that group pushed into the dangerous space between Peasants and Degradeds or Expendables . Furthermore, since between 95 and 97 percent of the Jewish state was illiterate at the time of Jesus, it must be presumed that Jesus also was illiterate, that he knew, like the vast majority of his contemporaries in an oral culture, the foundational narratives, basic stories, and general expectations of his tradition but not the exact texts, precise citations, or intricate arguments of its scribal elites." Crossan (pp. 25–26)

Interlude

The earthly Jesus
was not just a thinker with ideas but a rebel with a cause.
He was a Jewish peasant with an attitude,
and he claimed that his attitude was that of the Jewish God.
But it was, he said, in his life and ones like it that the
kingdom of God was revealed,
that the Jewish God of justice and righteousness was
incarnated in a world
of injustice and unrighteousness.
The kingdom of God was never just about words and ideas,
aphorisms and parables, sayings and dialogues.
It was about a way of life.
And that means it was about a body of flesh and blood.
Justice is always about bodies and lives, not just about
words and ideas.
Resurrection does not mean, simply, that the soul or spirit
of Jesus lives in the world.
And neither does it mean, simply,
that the companions or followers of Jesus live on
in the world.
It must be the embodied life that remains powerfully
efficacious in this world.
There is, then, only one Jesus, the embodied Galilean,
who lived a life of divine justice in an unjust world,
who was officially and legally executed by that world's
accredited representatives,

and whose continued empowering presence indicates,
for believers,
that God is not on the side of injustice, even (or especially)
imperial injustice.
There are not two Jesuses—one pre-Easter and
another post-Easter,
one earthly, another heavenly,
one with a physical and another with a spiritual body.
There is only one Jesus,
the historical Jesus
who incarnated the Jewish God of justice
for a believing community committed to such incarnation
ever afterward."[23]

[23]   John Dominic Crossan, *The Birth of Christianity; Discovering What Happened in the Years immediately After the Execution of Jesus*, (HarperSanFrancisco, 1998), p. xxx.

CHAPTER 4

Jesus: the Work of an Itinerant Sage

As long as you confine your choices to the alternatives that are presented to you in a given framework and do not think of questioning the framework itself, considering alternatives to that, you are not liberated.

—*Walter Kaufmann*

When we consider the impact of Jesus' work on the society of the Palestinian Province of the Roman Empire we have to begin with his birth. Please ignore, for a moment, the elaborate Nativity accounts in the Gospels of Matthew and Luke. They are parables about Jesus designed to explain the writers' conviction that the divine nature was in Jesus. Now look at two elements in the common traditions about Jesus: the implication that he was conceived out of wedlock and that his adoptive father, Joseph, was a carpenter. Admittedly these two assumptions are iffy. There is good reason, however, to consider them as significant because both of these factors are embarrassments for the One, the Person, whom his later followers claimed to incarnate the Godhead, to be "God of gods." The disgraceful allegations continue, however, to remain central in the tradition though somewhat sanitized and hallowed by the virgin-birth spin put on the story by Matthew and Luke.

Jesus had some kind of a brief involvement with John the Baptist and his apocalyptic movement. Jesus apparently broke off his relationship with John and embarked on a different kind of campaign. He chose the role of an itinerant sage moving from place to place, living among the lower classes as a healer and teacher, talking to them about a new vision of what could be. A new Empire of God is breaking into history. It is the diametric opposite of the empire of Rome. God, not Caesar, is the patron, and the poor are God's beloved clients. In this new empire, oppression is at an end. The poor know abundance, the hungry are fed, the sick and wounded are healed, and all people stand before God as pure and undefiled, honorable in the face of the holy of holies.

The stories of Jesus' birth as a bastard member of the artisan class placed him among the lowest of the low. He was most likely illiterate. Jesus chose to move among the poor and undertake a nonviolent campaign against the domination system and the oppressive elites. That he came from among the masses of the lower class and gained so much influence with them made his derisive, nonviolent subversion of the elite, ruling class a more powerful force than they could tolerate.

Here's what my friend, Greg Jenks, wrote to describe the power of Jesus' presence. (I have embellished his lines just a bit. prl)

> When Jesus was with them, peasants sickened by
> depression over their abysmal life situation were healed.
> When Jesus was with them, peasants blinded by despair
> saw visions of a new future.
> When Jesus was with them, starving peasants found
> abundance in sharing the little they had.
> When Jesus was with them, peasants shamed by imputed
> impurity found honor.

On the next page you will find my register of what Jesus did and what he had to say that undermined the cultural icons and mores of his day.

Cultural Norm	Jesus
Kinship was all-important to one's identity and being.	Jesus said, in many different ways, "You can choose your own family."
Purity was critical to a family's honor, and the lower classes were, by definition, impure and thereby excluded from true worthiness.	Jesus said, "You are forgiven—released from impurity. You are pure enough for God."
The dominating elites were blessed by God with riches and power in direct descent from the emperor. The lower classes were either marginal or expendable members of society.	Jesus said to the marginalized, "In God's new empire you are the special ones, the chosen, the elect."
Sin and impurity were supposedly the cause of the diseases suffered by the lower classes. Actually they suffered from illnesses caused by extreme poverty.	Jesus touched them in loving affirmation and acceptance and encouraged them to share with one another. They were healed.
Lower-class men and women were routinely abused and experienced themselves as victims.	Jesus encouraged them to follow his model and become freelance provocateurs of the new Empire of God.

In the process, Jesus ridiculed and made laughing stock of the elites at the top of the domination system, cutting away at their piety, hypocrisy, and arrogance.

When you think about it, Jesus' sense of himself borders on arrogant, certainly self-assured. Here was an illiterate man from almost the lowest class of society walking about as one who embodied the message he was bringing. He must have known himself as pure, as chosen, as healthy, as a member of a new family, as a healer, a teacher of holy wisdom. By all accounts he was charismatic.

Jesus broke mindsets. He thought outside the box of his culture. Jesus showed them that the ideas and givens that held the culture together were phantasms and fictions easily replaced by more generous and graceful values. Since the mind is culture ingested, he blew open minds and shook the foundations of a culture.

It is no wonder at all that Jesus was such a threat. He who shakes the roots of the belief system of the powers that be is far more threatening to them than a rebel with his armed revolutionary band. The rebel, in opposing the regime, actually affirms it as a system. If rebels are victorious, they soon enough become the dominators and reestablish the same or a more repressive government than the one they overthrew. The person who changes the underlying belief system creates a new order, a new way of being which causes grave discomfort for all those who are not open enough to comprehend it.

There is one other element of Jesus' program that threatens the status quo. Jesus moved among the marginalized people with whom he found himself at home. He healed them, told them his liberating stories, and gave them hope. He showed them how to experience the abundance of life in the midst of their poverty. He asked those who benefited from his work to establish outposts of the new domain of God in their homes by welcoming him and his friends to their tables. John Dominic Crossan calls this "open commensality." Our station in the social-class structure, he says, is most clearly indicated by those with whom we share our meals and our tables; the restaurants we frequent, the guests we invite, the dinners to which we are invited.

Jesus' message was that everybody of every social class is invited to the dinner tables in God's empire. All are considered equal in the world of Jesus' new vision. Jesus' program of open commensality is a declaration that the domain of God is classless.

As Jesus met the people of the rural villages, towns, and cities of Galilee, the Decapolis, and finally, Jerusalem, he moved with charismatic power . . .

1. First to heal the wounds and diseases caused by the domination system.
2. Then to tell them parables and talk about his vision of the new kingdom where God was immediately present and where all men, women, and children were peers.

3. Then to ask them to imitate him by adopting his lifestyle of simplicity, of sharing the abundance in poverty by eating with everyone regardless of their kinship or social class.
4. He then finally challenged them to follow him by becoming active in the nonviolent undermining of the domination system, manifested specifically by the Roman governors, their client overlords, and the Temple elite in Jerusalem.

All of those with whom Jesus spent his time were healed and heard the stories. Fewer had ears to hear and owned the vision for themselves. Only some of those began to live into the vision by imitating his lifestyle. And only a very few were able to sell all they had and follow him as itinerants into the nonviolent struggle against the domination-system mindset.

"The first disciples were invited by Jesus to a new location and a new vocation. They were called to join him on the road in a struggle to overturn the existing order of inequality and heal its victims."[24]

John Dominic Crossan summarizes it this way:

> The kingdom movement was Jesus' program of empowerment for a peasantry becoming steadily more hard-pressed through insistent taxation, attendant indebtedness, and eventual land expropriation, all within increasing commercialization in the expanding colonial economy of a Roman Empire under Augustan peace and a lower Galilee under Herodian urbanization. Jesus lived, against the systemic injustice and structural evil of that situation, an alternative open to all who would accept it: a life of open healing and shared eating, of radical itinerancy, programmatic homelessness, and

---

[24]   Myers, Ched et al., *Say to this Mountain: Mark's Story of Discipleship*, (Maryknoll: Orbis Books, 1996), p. 12.

fundamental egalitarianism, of human contact without discrimination, and of divine contact without hierarchy. He also died for that alternative. That is my understanding of what Jesus' words and deeds were all about. And I emphasize that it involved not so much Jesus' personal power as communal empowerment and not so much an idea of the mind as a life in the body. But notice that reciprocity of eating and healing is at the heart of the kingdom program and presence.[25]

Whatever level of response folks made to Jesus' presence, his healing, and his invitation to a new life, I consider them to be journeying on the Way he set out. If their response was nothing more than thanksgiving for his healing, or delight in his stories, folks became captivated by him. If they then take the next step and recognize their captivity in the domination system and determine to live differently within it by adopting simplicity and rejecting its violence, its fictions and lies, its rules, regulations, and mores, they are moving further along the Way. Even farther along the Way is a decision to leave or determinedly neglect family, friends, house, and home to live as Jesus lived; an itinerant sage. All are on the Way.

Jesus' radical program was short lived. The culture of the domination system was deeply embedded in the hearts and minds of his peers and followers. They struggled to integrate what he had said and done into their traditional ways of thinking and acting. But integration was nearly impossible. Gradually the radical nature of his program which sabotaged the domination system was eroded. It was not more than a generation before the uniqueness of his message and program was obscured and reinterpreted. By the time the Gospel of Matthew (70-80 CE) was written Jesus' words and work had been captured by the elites.

---

[25] Crossan, John Dominic, *The Essential Jesus: Original Sayings and Earliest Images*, (San Francisco: HarperSanFrancisco, 1994), p. 12.

Earlier on I cited John Dominic Crossan's estimation that "between 95 percent and 97 percent of the Jewish state was illiterate at the time of Jesus." The very fact that a life of Jesus was written means that scribes, who were members of the upper class, were taking over the Way and reshaping Jesus to reflect their own social situation. Most scholars, for example, believe that Matthew's Gospel was written to reflect the situation of Jewish synagogues in Diaspora who were following the new Way. So Matthew reconstructs Jesus to fit the history of Judaism. The Gospel's initial genealogy (Matthew 1:1 ff.) attempts to put Jesus in the lineage of David, the idolized king of the United Kingdom. The Sermon on the Mount (Matthew 5:1-29) is the first of five discourses the author of Matthew constructs as a parallel to the Torah or Pentateuch, the first five books of the Hebrew Bible. The teaching about Jesus is a new Torah, and it is not free of the violence of the domination system. (See Matthew 2:13-18)

Although the elites captured Jesus' message and program and made it their own, that is really only half the story. Jesus' vision about how the world might work differently, especially for the poor and marginalized, has been carried by word of mouth among the illiterate from one generation to the next.

Obviously we have no written record to tell us how the work of Jesus impacted his illiterate followers among the lower classes of the past twenty centuries. The official teaching about Jesus, that is the doctrines of the church, has been carried by the learned, privileged, male patriarchy. Very different ideas are carried in the folktales and notions of the illiterate, poor, and non-landed for whom Jesus is an empowering liberator. The windows at Chartres Cathedral, for example, were designed by the clerics to tell the Bible story to people who were illiterate. How the pictures in those windows were seen and interpreted by the poor is a hidden tale. The poor may get a different message than the one priests intended.

Even though the domination system has prevailed and the message of Jesus has been twisted to validate its excesses, his teaching has changed the way the world works. Even the elites, the upper classes, and those who conspire to maintain the domination system are different now because of Jesus' work.

I think there is evidence that the enlightenment and the industrial revolution are a product of Jesus' program. Nearly fifty years ago, in a brief paper prepared for the Center for the Study of Democratic Institutions, historian John U. Nef claimed that the Benedictine motto, "To work is to pray,"[26] represented the first time in human experience that intellect had been applied to physical labor. Over time similar applications of thought to human activity spread through Western culture and people began to operate as though the natural world was no longer sacrosanct. The notion that the natural world was independent of Divine Law led to the first serious explorations of the forces that governed the universe, the beginnings of science, and launched a new phenomenon that led to the first industrial revolution.

About four centuries ago, people started to break free of the divinely sanctioned iron hand of the elites. Now, in the twenty-first century, it is time to take off the last chains that bind culture in the domination system. We can shake the foundations of the domination system, bring about its collapse, and proclaim that a new day of peaceableness, abundance, and nonviolence is at hand. We can develop a new Way of human being that steadily moves to fulfill the vision of the illiterate itinerant sage from Nazareth. We hardly have the words to describe that New Human Being. We can best describe it by saying that it will not be a domination system, not hierarchical, not violent, with (distributive) justice for all.

---

[26]   Which, he said, was based on the fact that Jesus was a carpenter. Nef, John Ulric, *Civilization, Industrial Society, and Love; an occasional paper on the free society.* (Santa Barbara, Calif.) Center for the Study of Democratic Institutions (1961).

The assemblies of those committed to the New Human Being can adopt the circle way to practice and manifest a new social order in which all are peers. They will seek to find the healing and transformation of themselves so as to find the courage, trust, support, and grace to incarnate Jesus' program to liberate all of us from oppression step by step by:

- First working to heal the wounds and diseases caused by the domination system.
- Then telling Jesus' parables, making up new ones, and talking about his vision of the New Human Being where all men, women, and children are peers, and all are fed, clothed, and housed.
- Taking to themselves and helping others to adopt Jesus' lifestyle of simplicity, of sharing the abundance in poverty by eating with everyone regardless of their kinship or social class.
- Accepting Jesus' challenge to follow him by becoming active in the nonviolent undermining of the domination system, specifically the dominating power of international corporatism.

Tom Jackson is one of my good friends and a hero of the New Human Being. He founded the Order of Christian Workers [27] in Tyler, Texas and has done more to live out and support others to adopt the vision and lifestyle of Jesus than anyone I know. This is the statement of purpose of the OCW.

> As for us,
>> we will live this Journey in community,
>> risking to love and be loved,
>> stretching toward forgiveness and mutual respect,

---

[27]   You can contact Tom at journey@tyler.com. Send money! The OCW lives by begging.

growing in courage to be ourselves fully,
healing into wisdom and integrity,
transforming through hope,
recovering by grace.
We will listen intently,
serve gladly,
share openly,
trust joyfully,
live gratefully,
dream purposefully,
and celebrate exuberantly!

In the next chapter, I will tell you why the circle process is the Way to the New Human Being and incarnates the vision of Jesus' message and program in the twenty-first century.

CHAPTER 5

Why Jesus Circles Today?

The community of the New Human Being encompasses all
who attach themselves to it for the recovery of their freedom
and autonomy, their health and integrity, without any ranking
of class or achievement, without any permanent levels of
power and privilege.[28]

—*Herman Waetjen*

Gene S. Lovette was writing to an online discussion group which is exploring new paths for expressing a life based on the historical Jesus and had this commentary on the following text from the Gospel of Thomas 10.[29]

Jesus said, "I have cast fire upon the world, and look, I'm guarding it until it blazes."

---

[28]   Waetjen, Herman C., *A Reordering of Power: A Socio-Political Reading of Mark's Gospel*, (Minneapolis: Fortress Press, 1989), p. 100.

[29]   The Gospel of Thomas (or The Sayings Gospel) was found among the Nag Hammadi texts and is recognized by most scholars as a writing contemporaneous with the Gospels of Matthew, Mark, and Luke.

The kingdom of God is a commanding program that outlines a lifestyle based upon mutual reciprocity, i.e., healing for food and shelter, and its corollary of justice, compassion, and equality as the foundation of community government. Certain people heard Jesus and became ignited to subscribe to the program. These subscribers are the flame. Jesus enlists them to help HIM carry the vision forward and spread the flame, and ultimately create a fire that will cast a worldwide blaze. With that in mind, Jesus and his followers depart for Jerusalem, the hub of the world from which the blaze will light the world.

Unfortunately, unintended consequences arise. Jesus is executed in Jerusalem as a criminal.

A postlude: The dispersed followers are not up to nor capable of guarding the fire and nurturing it into a blaze. So it Petered Out-[30] and became the Church.

If you and I are to spread the flame of Jesus' vision and nurture it into a worldwide blaze, we need to develop a rich, contemporary vision of the New Human Being and embody that new being. We need to act out the vision and exemplify its characteristics. We need a nonviolent, collaborative process and system—a way that does not mimic the structures and patterns of the domination system. Our new understanding of Jesus in his own sociopolitical context requires in our day a new mode, a new system—a way that corresponds to Jesus' Way.

I am convinced that circles are the new alternative to the domination (patriarchal, hierarchical) system. Using the circle method we can find the healing we need. We can recognize our brokenness and

---

[30]   The pun is Lovette's.

name the disease that has been caused by our intellectual and spiritual captivity in domination-system cultural mindsets. We can be recreated as New Human Beings. We can then set out to create a new social order that moves all people closer to Jesus' vision of the just and peaceable kingdom of God.

We have so internalized the culture of the domination system that we have only one way to ameliorate our feelings of insecurity and fear. Again and again we revert to the use of power to win for ourselves the illusion of safety and security. Power over others and power over nature are our solutions to most problems. We "destroy" our political opponents. We "battle" cancer. We "wage war" on drugs. We "fight" forest fires. We "beat" the system. Collaboration is eschewed in favor of dialogue, debate, opposition, and conflict, and we say, may the best man win. Best, in this case, always means "the most powerful."

Jack Nelson-Pallmeyer says that the dominant religion today is not Christianity, not Islam, not Judaism, not Hinduism or Shintoism or any folk religion. It is the religion of violence.[31] As I write this the president of the United States and his neo-con managers[32] are celebrating the victory of a preemptive war against Iraq. It is unclear whether that war was waged in order to "free the Iraqis from oppression" or protect the USA from a paper tiger. In any case, the war has been won, and we are locked into a program to stabilize and reorganize a devastated, demoralized, and broken land. We are, therefore, like it or not, living in the time of the American imperium. Every sign indicates that the USA will attempt to dominate the economies and politics of the Middle East. Multinational corporations are eager to profit from the process of rebuilding Iraq, and the administration seems to be aiding them in every way possible. Except

---

[31]   In an address to the Robert McAfee Brown Seminar in Palo Alto, California, Nov. 2002 talking about a theme of his soon-to-be-published book.

[32]   Cheney, Perle et al.

for a few modern nuances, there isn't much difference between what the president is doing and what the Caesars did to expand their power and influence. In a column on the subject, Molly Ivins used this quotation from Benito Mussolini. "Fascism should more properly be called corporatism since it is the marriage of government and corporate power."[33] That's what we have, and it needs to be called by name: fascism or corporatism.

Thankfully we are living in the end days of the patriarchal church. In Western culture Christian churches have provided divine sanction to the domination system since 100 CE. As secularization begins to prevail, however, the religion of violence has to stand on its own; there are no more gods to sanction violence in their names. We read the canonical Scriptures of monotheistic religions and it is unambiguous; they have provided historical support for and validation of the domination system for thousands of years. Today, through advances in cultural anthropology, archeology, and biblical studies, we are able to see that most of what has been regarded as "Holy Scripture" is the product of the upper-class elites molding ancient stories and sagas into documents that validate their own hegemony.[34]

His victory at the Milvian Bridge outside Rome in 312 c.e. made Constantine I emperor in the West. According to legend, a cross and the words in hoc signo vinces (By this sign thou shalt conquer) appeared to him there, and he converted to the Christian faith. In 313 c.e. he issued the Edict of Milan, granting tolerance to Christians. As sole emperor, Constantine I began a program to put everything in his domain, under his control, and in right order. He proclaimed Christianity the official religion of the empire. He was distressed by

---

[33] And again in another column entitled, "The Road to Ideological Madness" in the Santa Rosa Press Democrat, August 10, 2003. Distributed by the Creators Syndicate.

[34] See Crossan, *The Historical Jesus*; Funk, Hoover and the Jesus Seminar; *The Five Gospels*; Finkelstein and Silberman, *The Bible Unearthed*.

the divergent Christian churches and theologies of his newly adopted religion, and as part of his program, he wanted them to model the unity and conformity he desired in everything. To help accomplish that aim, sometime between 325 and 330 c.e., he asked Eusebius, bishop in Caesarea, to select authoritative Christian texts from among the many available and compile fifty books of Scriptures for the fifty new churches he planned to build in Constantinople. We don't have the list of texts that then constituted Eusebius's Scriptures, but somewhat later he made a similar list of texts that look like those we read in what we call the New Testament. So it was that some writings became heretical and others lawful; that is authorized by the state. The domination system prevailed once again.

One strategy of dominators is to create the illusion that they are the only ones who can protect us from a series of hyped-up fears about which they are all too happy to inform us. By playing on our natural fear of dying, the domination system causes us to be fearful of one another, of strangers, of those different from us, of the future, of change, of imagination, and especially of flagrant vitality. Nearly as dreadful as the fear of death is the fear that our whole social system might collapse and leave us without cues and clues about what we can do to survive the chaos. The accepted order, the way things are, is sacrosanct. Any challenge to the ideas, adages, proverbs, and truisms that sustain society as it is, presents a most fearful prospect.

In the company of others in a circle we can learn to live beyond fear by engaging in free, frank, and deeply honest self-disclosure. That's the way we can unmask our fears and find they are mostly illusory. By relying on the wisdom of the group we can even find ways to live with radical uncertainty. We can learn to live with outrageous courage as Jesus did.

Because the domination system erodes our trust in one another, we don't trust the processes of life. That is why we try to dominate and control one another and nature, violently if it seems necessary, and we have the power to do so. In the nonthreatening milieu of circles we can disclose our inner life, our hopes and fears, and thereby learn that the true meaning of faith is trust. We can become free to live in trust. We can know peace and abundance in the face of all the threats, exigencies, and antinomies of human life including our own untimely and unseemly inevitable death.

The domination system arose when cultures accustomed to scarcity suddenly found great abundance. It was in the great river valleys at the time of the first agricultural revolution and the birth of civilization. The dominators wanted to control the warehouses stocked with surplus grain. Their goal was, of course, to dine well during the inevitable times of drought and famine. So they maintained and fostered the notion of scarcity in order to keep their power over those who produced the abundance, the farmers and peasants. As heirs of that culture of scarcity we still think there is never enough to satisfy our needs. The doctrine of scarcity tells us that the more you get the less is available for me. It says the pie is only so big, and there happen to be sixteen of us. We play first come, first served, and the six weakest ones will go hungry. The dominators get their needs met, and the others get leavings if there are any.

As we meet as peers in a circle we can recognize how we are aping the dominators and that much of our hunger is really our need to control what we think are scarce assets. With the support of our peers we will adopt a life of simplicity. Our next step will be a realization that sharing even scarce assets means shared abundance. Finally we will learn that dominators promote the idea of scarcity[35] in order to maintain power. We can undermine that power by living simply, producing more than we need and sharing it.

---

[35]   Advertising is one of the chief ways the notion of scarcity is perpetuated and promoted. We are constantly bombarded with messages that say we don't have enough of whatever product is being hustled.

One of the most devastating effects of the domination system is that it restricts our vision and saps our creative energy. We say, again and again: "Things never change." Or "The more things change the more they stay the same." Or "What do you expect of people? They never change."

With companionship in circles we can see how those "unchanging" truths are simply the product of domination-system minds. We can be liberated to make up new truths to serve a beautiful vision of a new way for the world to live.

A. The domination-system consciousness also constrains us to believe that we are not worthy. Since worthiness is a highly desirable state, we put ourselves under constant pressure to prove that we are worthy. Concomitantly, humiliation is one of the most feared of all experiences. We are squashed between our need to feel we are worthy and our fear of humiliation.

> This story is told about an expert hang glider pilot making an instructional videotape. The director mounted a video camera on the hang glider wing so it would focus on the pilot as he took off and went through a series of in-the-air maneuvers. The expert was fitted with a microphone so he could describe what he was doing as his body movements navigated the hang glider. Very shortly after takeoff he realized that he had forgotten to attach his safety harness, a potentially fatal oversight. But before he attempted to correct his mistake by attaching his safety harness, he reached far out beyond any margin of safety to switch off the camera. He did not want the videotape to record his mistake. His fear of death was less than his fear of humiliation.

A. The final gift of circles is that they become the source of our innate worthiness and our fortress against the little death of social humiliation. In circles we find the blessing of others: We come to honor and celebrate the power to live. That power is our natural heritage.

The author of the Gospel of John puts these words in Jesus' mouth, "I came that they may have life, and have it abundantly." (John 10:10)[36] This is not an authentic saying of Jesus. It is a parable about Jesus reflecting the experience of a community that was attempting to live in his Way nearly one hundred years after his death. That doesn't diminish the truth of the saying. In the company of others on the Way who are loving, supportive, nonjudgmental, and trusting, we can live abundantly in the most trying circumstances and life situations. For those whom Jesus touched with his healing power, abundant life also meant the hope, the promise, and realization of a society different from the oppression and poverty suffered under Pontius Pilate and his bosses in Rome. So it can be for us as in solidarity we work toward the final days of the domination system.

I believe that the circle process is the way to embody the vision and program of Jesus today. I know of no better way to emulate those local communities that learned from Jesus how to be whole and free and live in abundance. I call them Jesus Circles because it is in that format that the spirit of Jesus energizes small assemblies of equals helping one another enter into new lives in a new era of human being. The circle process can transform us into new people who embody distributive justice, the visionary "kingdom of God," in the midst of the unjust domination culture of this world. The culture we have inherited lives its domination way while we live wholly, healthily, powerfully, and abundantly in a new Way. Circles conform to Jesus' program in that they are "brokerless"—we teach each other and discover our power together as equals.

---

[36] While the writer may not have understood it this way, Jesus might have said, "It may sound ironic, but we all can have an abundant life in poverty."

We don't need to depend on experts, teachers, politicians, gurus, priests, or clergy to lead us. Circles are not hierarchical or patriarchal. Circles honor the truth that wisdom is discovered as a gift that comes when the offerings of each person are given and received with thanksgiving. Because we can go around and around the circle until we discover the hidden depths, circles are a healing, forgiving process that releases us from the oppression of one-upmanship into an empowering freedom that is a life-affirming process of support and comfort.

Just that life-affirming process happened to the staff of a nonprofit agency I worked with some years ago. Here's the story.

At twenty-eight, Frank Ryan was a retired steeplechase jockey. He didn't quit because he had lost the fire; that still burned mightily. The race stewards and doctors told him he had broken too many bones ever to ride again. Frank's passion shifted from winning races to a fierce dedication to the care, protection, and nurture of retarded children and adults. Since leaving the track, he had earned a master's degree and a Ph.D. and had nearly ten years working with agencies for retarded citizens. At the time I met him he had put in four very productive years as the director of a county association for retarded citizens.

I was earning my livelihood as an organizational development and personal consultant when I had a call from him one day, asking if I could help him with some problems in his agency. Frank explained that he had heard about me from a mutual friend. We made a date for lunch to explore the possibilities of my helping him. At lunch I heard his story. His staff was quietly rebelling against his leadership. He was mystified at what had eroded his leadership. He was very proud of the staff. He had hired most of them and really valued their work. Why were they upset?

We agreed to a contract, and I began my intervention with confidential interviews of each member of the staff; everyone, except the janitorial contractor. I quickly learned that Frank was riding the staff much like a steeplechase jockey—run faster, harder, and jump higher to get to the finish line. And to add further unrest, the staff felt that the finish line today seemed to be further in the distance than it was yesterday.

Frank and I had lunch again. I offered him a deal. I would help him if he was ready to take anything I or the staff dished out even if it turned out to be very painful, even humiliating. He agreed. He said he'd been hurt much more in his racing career than he could be hurt now. I wondered.

We planned a forty-eight-hour "retreat" for the entire staff. I booked a retreat center where we would have to do our own cooking. This was partly because of costs and partly by my design. I thought cooking and eating together would be a new and possibly enlightening experience for them. I sent out a memo and described the time schedule, the cooking arrangement, and what to bring. I promised that we would leave not later than 2:00 p.m. on the third day. I told them we were going to use the circle method as a way of identifying and hopefully solving the agency's problems. Tacitly everyone knew what the main problem was—except Frank.

The first round on our first evening was a safety check[37] and not everybody felt safe, but they had the courage to go on.

On the second round I asked each member to offer to the circle a brief story about how they had become involved in working on protective and educational services for the retarded. They were awed by what they learned about each other and discovered that many of their stories were very similar.

The third round of the evening was, "Is it possible to describe the worst setback you have experienced from the time you were ten

---

[37] See the next chapter for a description of the safety check.

years old?" Their sense of shared community deepened as they told and heard their stories of defeat, rejection, and grief.

The tasks I put them to in the first three rounds were designed as trust builders. Telling one's story and describing one's pains in a structured circle does two things at once. It levels the power structure we bring from our life in a domination system, and it enables members to identify more deeply with one another. The trust we experienced was a necessary foundation for honest self-disclosure during the remainder of the retreat.[38]

As a last task for the evening, we used the circle process to determine the cooking assignments for the next day.

The next morning our circle task was, "What's impeding us in our ability to get the job done?" As we went round and round, the offerings shifted from the very superficial to the more and more significant. We didn't use newsprint to post anything. No one took notes. The morning ended with a bit of tension in the air, but an increasing sense that we could trust one another.

The afternoon began on the same issue. On about the third round, Frank said, "I have the feeling that you guys don't really like me very much." The silence was deafening. There was a long pause, and the next person said something like, "It's that we love you and are frustrated by you." Period. All around the circle the offerings—now very clearly delivered to the center—were like that until it got to Frank's turn. "OK," he said, "give it to me straight. How am I screwing up? I want this agency to succeed, and I want you to be powerful to make it succeed. I will be open to hear anything you want to say to me. [He paused for a long

---

[38] I participated in the circle up to this point. That enabled me to be a part of the trust community. The next sessions were, however, none of my business. I was just an observer and sometimes guide.

moment.] And I promise that even if I hurt like hell I will not fire you or take retribution."

We only had time for two rounds because we had promised a couple of hours off before the supper cook team had to begin supper preparations. The two rounds were like pablum, soft and dissimulating responses. We broke with a mixture of feelings: "It feels good that we're making progress, but . . . we are really dancing around our true feelings."

The proverbial hit the fan in the circle after dinner. Frank was raked over the goals. With only one turn each time around, Frank had to hear it without defending himself. Finally he broke down and, in a long offering, talked openly about his fears, his uncertainties, and how he had always geared up, knuckled down, and doubled his efforts when things got difficult. It was the classical, "When the going gets tough the tough gets going." He also revealed, though not consciously, that he was a loner and had never relied on help from anyone.

The next round went, "Right!" "Correct." "Yes." "That's what we thought." And the round after that was, "How can we help you change so we can help you and do what we want to do?" It was a bit of an emotional bash. Frank obviously and emotionally experienced their respect and love for him. He later told me that he had never before known what that was like. His life had been too hard for true feelings of affection.

The next morning was devoted to decisions and plans for the future. Frank couldn't ride his high horse. With these people, with this staff, he had learned it wouldn't work. And because with the circle method, he only had the same allotment of leadership time as every other person on the staff.

That forty-eight-hour circle process empowered a radical change in Frank and in that agency staff. They went away as new people knowing an abundance of life that had until then been concealed under a domination system.

We are all living in a domination system. So the circle process has the same effect everywhere. Time after time, in all kinds of settings, with all kinds of folks, it turns out that the participants leave feeling affirmed and powerful. They leave with high sense of accomplishment. It is an abundant way toward a New Human Being.

Interlude 2

Scene 1: The Domination-System Process

Setting: The vestry meeting to elect a junior warden.

As the third item on the agenda, the call for nominations results in three people being nominated—Wendy, Shirley, and Jim.

On the first secret ballot, Jim is eliminated decisively.

Someone suggests that Wendy and Shirley be excused from the room so the others can talk. The discussion evolves into a polite and restrained, but serious conflict between the evenly divided supporters of each nominee.

There is a call for another ballot. Wendy and Shirley return to the meeting for secret ballot number 2.

Wendy and Shirley, having talked while out of the room, announce their joint decision to withdraw. All the others reject that option. Someone suggests George, who happens to be absent. That idea is met with derision and is gone in two seconds.

The clerk's count of the second secret ballot shows it's a tie. What do we do now?

One of the older members suggests that the rector and senior warden chose one of the two to be the junior warden.

The rector reacts quickly. She sees that suggestion as a no-win for her and decides they must take time to pray about it. Without stating her fears or even drawing another breath, she says, "Let us pray." Her prayer is a long rehash of the situation and its history (which God should already know if He is an interventionist God, and which everyone in the room already knows). She concludes by asking God to make his will known to them.

After the amen, the senior warden, his patience at an end, says, "It's Wendy. What's the next item on the agenda?"

No one leaves happy. Everyone feels defeated and frustrated. In the end everyone has acquiesced to the power of the senior warden. The vestry process this year is off to its usual terrible start.

Scene 2: The Abundance System Circle Process

Setting: The vestry meeting to select a junior warden.

The rector and senior warden ask that the vestry use the circle process to select a junior warden.

The first round is a brief check-in during which each member responds to the question: How have things been for you in the last couple of weeks?

The second round and subsequent rounds respond to the question: Who is being called to be junior warden for this year?

During the second round several of the members simply withdrew from consideration for personal reasons. Two members, Wendy and Shirley, each said they thought they could be the junior warden and that they could manage the process. One member suggested that they consider George who was not present.

In the third round members offered their thoughts and feelings to the center of the group. Several offered the opinion that it is unfair to George to select him when he isn't present. While most of the third-round offerings are reflections on the nature of the job of junior warden, it is apparent that the vestry is almost evenly divided as to which of the two would make the best junior warden. When it is Wendy's time to offer her thoughts, she is both soft spoken and eloquent in describing her vision of the junior warden's tasks in the coming year.

In the fourth round, the fifth person in the circle is Shirley. She looks for a moment at Wendy, turns her eyes to the center, and says, "It has become clear to me that the spirit is calling Wendy to be our junior warden this year, and I suggest we call on her to accept the responsibility." She touches the next person sunwise. He is silent for a moment and then says, "I'm not as clear about the spirit's leading as you are and want to hold the decision open for a bit more discussion." The next person offers the opinion that while she isn't clear about the spirit, she is clear that Wendy ought to take the job. Wendy is next in the circle and passes. There is one more round, and during that round everyone expresses confidence that the wisdom of the group falls on Wendy.

Everyone goes away feeling joy, peace, and a sense of well-being. The vestry year is off to a great start.

CHAPTER 6

The Circle Process in Detail

Our determination to pursue truth by setting up a fight between two sides leads us to believe that every issue has two sides—no more, no less: If both sides are given a forum to confront each other, all the relevant information will emerge, and the best case will be made for each side. But opposition does not lead to truth when an issue is not composed of two opposing sides but is a crystal of many sides. Often the truth is in the complex middle, not the oversimplified extremes.[39]

—*Deborah Tannen*

I have focused on coming to a deeper understanding of the Jesus of history and seeking ways to follow in his steps. I hope that you will make a decision to explore your own future by becoming part of a circle with that focus.

The circle process will guide you into a much more satisfactory experience than you have had in any other group format. And when

---

[39]   Tannen, Deborah, *The Argument Culture: Stopping America's War of Words*, Third Paper Edition, (Ballantine Books, February 1999) p. 3.

your circle has been together for a year or two, you will find that you are living an abundant life that is both in the midst of and transcending the domination culture. You may also be surprised to find that you are acting as agents of the transformation to the New Human Being.

Starting a new group:

What kind of a group do you want it to be?

> A study group?
> A personal or spiritual growth group?
> A support group?
> An action group?
> A family meeting?
> A group of friends experimenting with being together
> in a new way?

That decided, you need to identify the people whom you would like to be a part of the group. It's best if the folks you gather are people who will accept your leadership for the first few weeks of the group's life. You can make it very clear that you want to convene the group and that you want it to follow a new process that may be different than your invitees may have known before. You probably should make it a condition that the group follows your suggested process (the circle process) for the first six weeks.

Invite your chosen friends to join you. Experience, over a long period of time, shows that a group needs about six sessions to jell and become effective for its members. And weekly meetings are best. If you can't manage weekly, try for every other week at the same time and same place. Neither the time nor the place is significant except for the convenience of the members. Our Men's group met at 6:30 a.m. on Saturdays, and we ended without fail by 8:00 a.m. A firm start time that is respected by all the members will make for a positive experience. Waiting around for latecomers is always a downer. So try to get agreement that you all will be there to start on time. A firm ending time is also very important. That respects every person's life outside of the group. Your initial invitation should make clear that you will be starting and ending on time every time.

The place for your meeting needs to be somewhat comfortable and large enough so that the members can sit in a circle. Your living or family room at home or a meeting room in a public library, church, lodge hall, or office are equally good. With a small circle, you might meet at a local coffee shop. You can even sit on hay bales in a barn if that's a comfortable venue for your members. Try not to sit around a table. Tables tend to be rectangular, and rectangles seem to have a subtle negative effect on the process. A table is also a barrier that impedes trust building. Circles that are very experienced with the process will not be bothered by tables, but try not to have the first six or eight meetings seated at a table

The norms and rituals of the circle process ensure that all the members are equally involved in the life of the group. The wisdom and insight of every member is essential to discovering true wisdom for our lives at this time.

The process is a ritual, which one dictionary defines as "a prescribed form or order of conducting a religious ceremony" or "a detailed method or procedure faithfully or regularly followed." The circle method is not a religious rite, but following the ritual ensures the maximum benefit from the process. Folks like us who grew up in the domination system of the Western world need significant discipline to suppress our competitiveness and our need to be one-up.

Here are the circle norms.

The group gathers and the usual pleasantries exchanged, and everyone takes a seat in a circle, the order doesn't matter at all.

1. Silence and centering

It is well to have a brief period of silence and centering, a time to let go of the anxieties, noise, and distractions we usually carry with us all day long. The silent time may be a guided centering exercise like a simple reminder that following and watching one's breathing is perhaps the simplest centering method. One guided exercise I have used frequently is what I call a "safety check." I ask the members of the group to check their bodies to see if they feel any discomfort of pain that will keep them from being totally present here and now. I ask them to look around the room and check to see if they feel safe and secure in this place. I ask them to look at each person in the circle to see if they feel comfortable with these people. On the very, very rare occasion when someone says they don't feel safe or comfortable, I ask them to take a moment to do something about their discomfort. Sometimes a suggestion that the discomfort be put aside for the time being will work. Other times it might mean taking off a sweater. Usually the problem can be easily solved, and we are able to go to the next step.

2. Check-in sunwise

Check-in is always the next step. Members respond to questions like these:

> Can you tell us how it's been for you since the last time
> we were together?[40]
> Can you tell us what's happened in your life since our
> last meeting?

---

[40] The renowned family therapist, Virginia Satir, rarely asked a direct question of her clients. She always framed her question with, "Can you tell me about ..." This allows the respondent to say, if they choose, "No, I can't tell you about that?" Usually, however, any defensiveness is dissipated by the permissive way the inquiry is framed.

The responses always move from one person to the next sunwise (clockwise—to the left) around the circle. Whenever the need arises it is perfectly acceptable to pass and let the next person on the left begin.

My experience has shown that the best way to tell the person on your left that you are finished with your contribution is to lightly touch that person. The touch allows for folks to have periods of silence to be sure they have said all that's important before giving the next person his or her turn to address the circle. It also avoids awkward silences caused by the uncertainty of knowing whether or not the speaker is finished. Some people who are experienced with the circle process advocate the use of a "talking stick" that is passed from one person to the next. The stick may be a very simple object, not necessarily a stick at all, or it may be a ceremonially decorated stick. I have never known anyone to be uncomfortable with a light touch, and a touch may contribute to a deeper sense of community and trust.

The touch also enables a response that is wholly silent or is a "pass." It is always necessary to allow members to pass when their turn comes. Somehow, given our culturally infused sense of inadequacy, it seems embarrassing to have to say, "I pass." Given our sense of built-in unworthiness that's too often felt as "I'm a dummy and I have nothing to add." Or "I am too stupid about this whole subject."

3. Identify the topic for the session or the issue to be resolved and the agreed time for ending

It may be that the circle has a preset agenda, like studying the third chapter of *The Gospel of Jesus* or determining how to respond to a call for a demonstration against some political policy. Or it may be that the circle is the board of a local church that must decide on which candidate is to be their new minister. If there is a specific task or agenda, it should be noted and addressed following the check-in. The time for adjournment is also stated.

4. Offer your gift to the center of the circle

Another very important ritual is that all contributions are made to the center of the circle. It is as though I am offering my report, my thought, my fantasy, my dream, this part of my wisdom to all of you by placing it in the center of our circle. When it is offered to the center of the circle, any kind of comment is acceptable and is offered without embarrassment, self-consciousness, or judgment.

"Make and keep eye contact" is the advice usually given in training sessions for public speakers, managers, and leaders. That's good advice if you are addressing a crowd of hundreds seated in an auditorium or classroom. It's very good advice for anyone trying to make their way in a domination system because it is the way predators behave. Predators, animals that chase and kill, have eyes in the front of their skulls, the better to see their prey. Prey animals have eyes on the side of their skulls, the better to be on the lookout for predators.

So we, humans, are by nature predators, and predation is at the root of the dominance game and the domination system. Strong eye contact shows our power against or over the other. Downcast eyes and the side of the neck exposed to the other are signs of submission and surrender. The only situation in which this is not true is with lovers, when they gaze deeply into one another's eyes in adoration, worship, and desire. Then eye contact is the sharing of souls.

> I will never forget an experience our family had while staying in a campground in Keam's Canyon on the Hopi Reservation. During the day, while we were attending the Homecoming Dance on First Mesa, our tent was shot through with arrows. The tent was ripped in several places, and there was one telltale arrow inside it. We went up to the Hopi Police Station and made a report. Early in the evening a Hopi police officer came down to investigate, and we invited him to have some refreshments. As we sat and talked, he never once made

eye contact with any of us. He simply looked out in an unfocused way—a kind of gentle looking. The Hopi tend to believe[41] that when you look into another's eyes you are looking into their soul. None of us had permission to look into another's soul that evening. When we did get a report back from the Hopi Police, they had concluded that some "renegade Navajo kids" had made an attack on us "white ghosts." Our meeting with the Hopi police officer was in sharp contrast with what we might have experienced with our own hometown cops.

Offering your wisdom or insight to the center of the circle is not a submissive act. It is collaborative. It recognizes that my wisdom is very limited and the whole wisdom is the exponential sum of all our little wisdoms.

5. No cross talk

Another norm of the circle process is that there is no cross talk. It makes no difference how much I need to respond to your comment. I have to wait for my turn in the circle. Your statement was made to the group as a whole, and I am only one member of the group, even if you seem to have made a specific criticism of me or my point of view.

Deborah Tannen has campaigned against "a pervasive warlike atmosphere that makes us approach public dialogue, and just about anything we need to accomplish, as if it were a fight."[42] She writes: "It is a tendency in Western culture in general, and in the United

---

[41]   I say "tend to believe" because some Hopi are now socialized into the domination culture.

[42]   Tannen, Deborah, *The Argument Culture: Stopping America's War of Words*, Third Paper Edition (Ballantine Books, February 1999), p. 10.

States in particular, that has a long history and a deep, thick, and far-ranging root system. It has served us well in many ways but in recent years has become so exaggerated that it is getting in the way of solving our problems. Our spirits are corroded by living in an atmosphere of unrelenting contention—an argument culture.

"The argument culture urges us to regard the world—and the people in it—in an adversarial frame of mind. It rests on the assumption that opposition is the best way to get anything done: The best way to explore an idea is to set up a debate; the best way to cover the news is to find spokespeople who express the most extreme, polarized views and present them as "both sides"; the best way to settle disputes is litigation that pits one party against the other; the best way to begin an essay is to oppose someone; and the best way to show you're really thinking is to criticize and attack. The war on drugs, the war on cancer, the battle of the sexes, politicians' turf battles—in the argument culture, war metaphors pervade our talk and shape our thinking."[43]

We can easily substitute "domination-system culture" for her term "argument culture." The metaphors of war and its violence permeate our daily discourse. We must find a new way to get to the wisdom that can lead us to the just and nonviolent domain of New Human Being.

It is very difficult to have an argument with another member of the circle when each person must take his or her turn in order, and there is no cross talk. What tends to happen is that interpersonal issues simply fade way by the time it's my turn to respond to your statement I had objected to so emotionally and strenuously only moments ago. New data, new feelings, new thoughts have intervened, and the energy has shifted away from conflict and toward shared wisdom. So, no cross talk.

---

[43] Tannen, Op.cit. p. 3.

I think the act of listening—dangerous though it may
be when absorbing the spirit and statement of another—
even when we do not agree with him or her—is an act
of love.

6. Confidentiality—what's said in this room stays in this room

Because the effectiveness of the circle process depends upon mutual
trust and the freedom to speak with utmost honesty, it is essential to
agree to strict confidentiality among members of the group. We all
agree to keep what is said in this circle in this group and not speak
of it or mention it to others.

I encountered a very awkward violation of this principle one
day many years ago. A friend had confided in me that he was a
member of an Addicts Anonymous Group. Months later, as we
were working together, he casually asked me if I knew the
Reverend So-and-So. Whoops! I not only knew him, he had once
been my boss. I answered by saying no more than "yes," but my
friend blurted out, "I shouldn't have said that." He had broken
trust with his peers in his recovery group. I had suspected that
my former boss was abusing drugs but no real data that
supported my guess. Now I knew and should not have learned it
this way.

7. An Ending Ritual

Ending any kind of a group meeting means that relationships are
partially severed; a passage is made to a new set of relationships, a
new time of life. In one sense we bury one part of our lives to be born
again in another. Good-byes are what that contraction really means,
"God by ye," That is "God be with you while we are apart." It is as
though we say, "In what we have just shared in this group we have
known safety, comfort, love, acceptance, and it is good. Now there is
a more cruel and precarious world into which we must move, and I

want you to be safe, comfortable, loved, accepted, and have it all be good."

The ending of a circle shouldn't be like that awful period of anticipated separation between a teenager and parent. The parent says, "I love this kid and the kid loves me and his/her impending departure for college or some other distant place is going to be really hard on us." The kid is saying, "I don't want to leave home, but I have to, or I'll never grow up. I love my mom and dad, and I don't know how I'll be able to get along without them, but I have to. God, I hate this."

In order to spare themselves the heartbreak of separation, both parents and kids become silent and withdrawn, angry and hateful toward one another. To help them separate, they need to feign disgust with one another. Both parents and the kid are pretending, "What a relief to be rid of you." The same sort of undermining phenomenon can occur when people in less intimate relationships separate. To assuage our dismay when we are ending a group meeting, we tend to discount what we mean to each other. Structuring a ritual time for separation is, therefore, very important to the continuing health of the group and its members.

When the time comes to end circle session, you have a number of options.

- You may do one more round, asking for final comments like, what this session has meant to me, or what I have received from you during this session, or I am thankful for this evening because . . .
- You may do a final round in which each person makes an action commitment like, what I will do this week to to live more freely, or undermine the domination system, or to act out what I want the world to be like.
- A final round might be one in which each member says a prayer for the person on his/her left. (Reach out and touch them as you pray.)

- You may share a meal. It maybe a simple ritual in which each member takes one pinch of a piece of bread or a roll in turn sunwise. It may be that you break out of the circle to share a full meal. For many people who have a long history with the Eucharist, the ritual meal that commemorates the presence of Jesus with his people, a form of the communion service might be most meaningful. John Dominic Crossan has said that our social status is most revealed by the companions with whom we choose to share a meal. If your circle fellowship is characteristic of the just and nonviolent New Human Being, you will want to eat together.

Listen to Jack Nelson-Pallmeyer. "Through these rituals [the Eucharistic rites] we remember and recommit ourselves to the powerful example of Jesus' nonviolent witness to the compassionate Spirit of God reflected in his public ministry of exposing oppressive systems, in his inclusive table practice of shared meals, and in his vision of an alternative order rooted in justice in which all would be fed. By sharing a meal communally or by receiving communion together we celebrate the nonviolent presence of God in daily bread and express our commitment to be in solidarity with those who hunger for real food and spiritual nourishment.

"We can preserve the tradition linking a community meal with the betrayal of Jesus by communicating clearly that Communion is a solidarity meal in which we declare God's intent and our commitment that all be fed. Communion should always be understood as a risky, subversive act. It challenges systems that accept hunger as an acceptable cost of progress. It is in food and drink offered equally to everyone that the presence of God and Jesus is found. But food and drink are the material bases of life, so the Lord's Supper is a political criticism and economic challenge as well as a sacred rite."[44]

---

[44] Nelson-Pallmeyer, Jack, *Jesus Against Christianity: Reclaiming the*

8. About Leadership

I continue to have a hard time thinking about how to name the
function of guidance in circles. All of the usual terms are dominance
system words—leader, chairman, even convener. The definition of
leader I like best was invented in the Group Life movement some
fifty years ago. They understood leadership as an evocative function
that sought the maximum potential from any group process. They
called it maieutic leadership. The word maiuetic is derived from the
Greek word for midwife and suggests the sense of gently easing out
what is coming naturally in the first place. The function of the person
selected to midwife a circle is to help the group keep to its rituals and
move it along to the next stage of its process; that is to begin the
session, to identify its task, set the time, to keep to the norms, etc.
Finally the responsibility of that person in task-oriented group is to
be the decision maker if the group cannot reach a harmonic outcome
about an issue under consideration.

Though it may sound a bit ostentatious to you, I am going to suggest
the title "Wisdom Keeper" for the guiding and midwife-like function
in a circle. If, for example, during the process of check-in one member of
the circle reveals a new life issue—a death in the family or a bad medical
diagnosis—that might require attention from other members of the
group, it is the job of the Wisdom Keeper to suggest at least one round
(and maybe two or three) of response.

During the session, the Wisdom Keeper may need to remind members
of the norms or intervene gently if one member starts cross talking.
When it is time to end the circle session, the Wisdom Keeper suggests
an ending ritual if this has not already been planned.

In decision-making circles the role of the Wisdom Keeper is more

---

Missing Jesus, (Harrisburg, PA: Trinity Press International , 2001), p.
342. (Italics mine.)

significant. The Wisdom Keeper is the ultimate decision maker when consensus seems impossible in the time allotted. When the circle is unable to resolve an issue, the members agree to abide by the Wisdom Keeper's final decision and act on the necessary steps to implement the solution.

On many occasions I have been amazed by the ability of a circle to come to a difficult decision within the time allotted. There is a kind of mysterious magic that empowers a group assembled in a circle to make a very difficult decision in only an hour when that's all the time there is to be had. I have been involved on a few occasions, however, when that did not happen. In those cases we had previously decided to accept the Wisdom Keeper's decisions as the will of the circle and that all of us would abide by that decision. Each time we did that, the results were excellent. Everyone seemed to be satisfied that we had done our best work and unreservedly supported the outcome.

The role of the Wisdom Keeper should rotate among members of the group, and one final task of the group may be to decide who will keep the wisdom at the next session. To be truly trusting in the process, however, the next Wisdom Keeper should be chosen by lot. It is the best way to expunge the unconscious use of hierarchical criteria.

The circle way also works in crisis situations like the one below. The story has been fictionalized to protect the chief actors in the real life story.

> The pastor of St. Barnabas Church was a very liberal theologian who had a reputation in the community for his open-mindedness and social concerns. Over the course of years he had begun to eat away at the hierarchical structure of his congregation and had introduced the circle way to study groups, the Christian Education Commission, and the board of trustees. The board had used the circle way to elect its officers, set program priorities, and adopt the annual budget. They

were experienced in the Way and found it a harmonic model for other groups in the church.

The crisis that potentially rocked the congregation was a longtime brewing. It began, as most do, in the unresolved issues that people bring from their past into the present. The organist and one of the trustees had such issues and were trying to work them out. Unfortunately they tried to do it with one another. They "fell in love."

Will, the trustee, sang in the choir, a married father of two young kids and a very successful businessman. Ellen, the organist, was married to a denominational executive—an ordained minister overseeing a number of congregations. They had two teenagers who are both active in the youth group.

For some time the signs of more-than-normal intimacy between them had been evident to those that had eyes to see. Eventually it became a bit of an embarrassment when Will and Ellen were seen holding hands and whispering in one another's ears. The couple talked to an elder whom they both trusted. His counsel was to be candid with their friends and with members of the congregation about their plan to divorce their spouses and marry.

So it was that the rumor mill processed the truth. Among the first to hear were the pastor and members of the board of trustees. Calls heated the phone lines to the pastor's office. "Scandal in the church's leadership!" "Adultery in high places!" "Terrible!" "Something must be done!"

The pastor sat down with Ellen and Will. They were insulated by their love for one another from any awareness of the threat their relationship posed to the community. They were being "open and honest," and if that was a problem, it wasn't theirs. The pastor did, however, get them to agree to come to a meeting with the board of trustees and two former presidents of the congregation, both of whom were mightily upset by the situation.

An evening meeting was set and the board of trustees, the clergy, the former presidents, and Ellen were in a circle in the same room. Neither Will's nor Ellen's spouses were members of the congregation and declined to attend the meeting. Some of those present were angry, others perplexed and confused, others offended. Everyone was scared, especially the pastor and the lovers. Ellen and Will held hands.

The pastor began by saying that they would use the circle way, and the meeting would last no more than two hours. He asked for a period of silence in which to invoke the power of the Holy Spirit's wisdom to help them find a creative way for the community. Then he asked for a safety check. In that round everyone felt safe and ready to begin. The pastor began the first round by addressing the center, speaking about his trust in the circle process and his confidence in the wisdom that would emerge. The first round was characterized by all the expressions one might expect. Each person addressed the center, and emotions ran deep. Round and round they went for over an hour, and with each round emotions stilled and wisdom began to emerge.

Finally one of the older members of the group said, "I think we've got this figured out." As the round proceeded, each person expressed a sense that they and the congregation were just fine. All had made confession, experienced forgiveness, and felt reconciliation. The way ahead had been discovered. Typical with this group, the circle way ended with each person saying a brief prayer for the person at his or her left.

No decisions had been made. No one attempted to summarize the situation. No plan was presented or adopted. The group went home and lived out the wisdom. Healing could begin. Wholeness would be restored. The grief and pain in Ellen's and Will's families would go on as long as the mourning must go on when a death or other awful separation occurs. The difference in this crisis was that both families had loving, wise, and faithful support from those who sat in that circle way that momentous evening.

I can hear you ask, "Doesn't the circle process take too much time?" Yes, sometimes it does.

Our concern about time and efficiency arises out of our familiarity with domination-system problem solving and decision making. We like efficiency and speed. We sometimes secretly admire the speed with which dictators and CEOs can make decisions affecting millions. I was recently having lunch aboard an Amtrak train headed for Seattle, and my tablemates were a fascinating and well-traveled couple from Wales. They had recently visited their son, a businessman in Moscow. They complained that Moscow had run down since their previous visit before the collapse of the Communist state. They then generalized and said that they much preferred to travel in dictatorships. Things were much more efficient, they said.

Those fast and efficient decisions made by powerful elites are often, however, the cause of manifold misery to thousands and enormous hidden costs to the systems involved. And the use of coercion and force is sometimes necessary to affect the elites' desired outcome.

When decisions are made through a circle process, things are different. By the time a circle senses a decision, the soundness of it, the commitment to it, and the energy required to implement it have already been built into the process.

You can choose domination-system efficiency and the erosion of confidence, loyalty, commitment, and energy that often follow along its path; not to mention the odious sanctions that are imposed when the decision is not working. Or you can choose to take a few more minutes or hours in a circle and have the outcomes be abundantly satisfactory.

CHAPTER 7

Designing the Circle Process for Large Assemblies

Jesus said, "To listen to you or to listen to me is not to hear us but to hear the word of God who sent us both."[45]

Let me suggest four different scenarios in which the circle process might be used for large assemblies.

1. St. Andrew's Church is approaching the one hundredth anniversary of its foundation. It is a medium-sized congregation with an average Sunday attendance of 210 people, not including children. The church leaders want to have everybody participate in planning the centennial celebration. How can they get everyone involved?

2. Surprisingly fifty-eight people have registered for our six-week Lenten Study Group when in past years only twenty or so was the maximum registration. We are afraid some of the more extroverted, articulate, self-styled experts will dominate the discussion. We want everyone

---

[45] Crossan, John Dominic, *The Essential Jesus: Original Sayings and Earliest Images*, (Edison, NJ: Castle Books, 1994), p. 37.

to have an opportunity to participate. How can we meet these goals?

3. Our social-service agency which has a staff of sixty-three professional and support people has been deeply shocked by the seemingly random murder of one of our most loved members. We want to talk about her death and our loss and have everyone involved. Is there a way we can do this?

4. We think that about forty-six members of our extended family will be coming to our triennial family reunion. In the last three years our most revered elder, our matriarch, Grandma Willson, has slipped into Alzheimer's, and we want to set up a time when we can grieve our loss of her without staging a kind of funeral.

Here's the way to organize the circle process for large assemblies.

1. Describe to the entire assembly exactly what the process will be. Some people will get it immediately. You can be sure that others will be dumb as posts and think of all kinds of stupid questions and may want to ask them. Without being rude or demeaning, ask them simply to trust the process and they will get clear as it moves along.

2. Divide the assembly into approximately equally sized small groups of five to twelve. I think it was E. F. Schumaker who said, "Jesus was right about one thing. Any group larger than twelve is doomed."

    The method you use to set the groups can vary. One way is to have the members count off and ask all the ones to meet in one corner, twos in another corner, threes in another, etc. Another is to ask groups to cluster with the people sitting around them. The requirement is that every chair be in as true a circle as possible. Some people naturally want to sit back from the group. Ask them to draw into the circle, emphasizing that "passing" is always an option for every person.

3. Ask the members to do a safety check. (Refer back to chapter 6)
4. Go over the norms for the circle process. (Refer back to chapter 6)

When I am acting as the guide for a large assembly I ask that the first person to speak is the person with his or her back to one wall of the room. That ensures a clear start and saves the old problem of "No, you go first."

5. The first two or even three rounds are trust-building rounds.

In the first round I always ask people to say their names and some seemingly innocuous thing like their place in the birth order.

Before the second round I may ask them to think quietly about the worst thing they have ever done, and then the second worst thing they have ever done, and then the third and even the fourth. I tell them never to tell anyone the worst thing they have done. Then I ask them if it is possible in this round to tell the group the third or fourth worst thing they have ever done. I repeat that they can pass, or tell the tenth worst thing. It is an amazing trust builder, because it is safe and self-disclosing at the same time.

6. Introduce the subject or topic for the assembly. Here's how I would introduce the topic for the four examples above.

   1. St. Andrew's Church approaching the one hundredth anniversary of its foundation.
      Think for a few moments about this question: As you look back over what you know of the history of St. Andrew's, what strengths might we want to honor in this celebration? In the next fifteen minutes

go round and round on this topic, sharing your ideas with your circle.

2. For a six-week Lenten Study Group on Marcus Borg's book, Meeting Jesus Again for the First Time. (Preparation for the first session of the study group was to read the introduction and chapter 1 of the book.)

Thinking back to your first reading chapter 1, can you share your initial impression of what Borg presents?

3. Our social-service agency staff has been deeply shocked by the seemingly random murder of one of our most loved members.

Please share with your circle where you were when you first heard about Helene's murder. When you have all told about this, talk in the next round about your first reaction to the news.

4. Our extended family needs to grieve our loss of Grandma Willson to Alzheimer's.

Can you tell the members of your circle what worries you most about Grandma Willson's condition?

In some circumstances you may simply let the circles go round and round on their own until an allotted time is up. In other cases, as for example, in planning the centennial celebration, you may want to shift into topics like, "What dreams and fantasies do you have about this celebration?" or "How much time, energy, and money should we devote to the celebration?"

Decision making in large groups or assemblies is one of the most exciting applications of the circle process. As in the fictional case of St. Andrews (and perhaps also in the case of Helene's murder) it is wise to make certain there is time for two or more final steps in the process.

At a preset time each small-circle group should select one member to carry their wisdom to the entire assembly. That may take a few rounds before it is clear about which member that will be. Those chosen might be called syndics, a term that signifies a representative to a large assembly. I may sound picky here, but the terms we normally use for this kind of function carry with them the suggestion of domination.[46] I am trying to avoid that by finding different terms that free us from domination-system intimations.

The syndics gather in a circle with their small-circle members sitting behind them. Then they offer their sense of their small circle's wisdom to the whole assembly by placing it in the center of the syndic circle.

If a specific decision is necessary, as, for example, the maximum expenditure for a centennial celebration must be set; the syndics go round and round until the decision is made.

I can hear you saying again, "Doesn't this take too much time?" My answer is maybe, maybe not. Time is not the only consideration. Sure, we are all pressed for time, but we are also pressed for joy, for satisfaction, for feelings of mutual accomplishment, for the abundance that comes when we are in full concert with our sisters and brothers.

In the circle process it is rare that anyone comes away with bad feelings, of having been overridden, of being vetoed out or run over. Members experience the abundance of being heard and attended to, listened to and honored. And finally, the product of their mutual wisdom is honored and enacted with all of their spiritual, mental, and physical energy engaged.

---

[46] "Leader" is up. "Member" is down.

CHAPTER 8

Getting Deeper into the Way of Jesus: Some Session Topics

The key to self-fulfillment is commitment to a life that builds
abundance and beauty and distributive justice in the world.
—PRL

I offer these stories, sayings, parables, and aphorisms as Jesus Circle topics. After "check-in," the piece can be read by the Wisdom Keeper, and, after a period of silence, each person responds in turn until the time has expired.

✧ The fundamental mode

    ✧ The fundamental mode of a follower of Jesus is to live into the new age, the domain of the New Human Being, the new era, the new humanity, before anyone else is there.

    ✧ The fundamental mode of a follower of Jesus is to live with courage; that is, to live beyond death into new life, abandoning all that is for what is to become. Going without staff or purse or extra coat is living over the edge into the death of today and the beginning of tomorrow.

✠   ✠   ✠

Those who have nothing to protect or save them from the next tragedy or setback are most prepared to experience the wonder of a more just, egalitarian, and peaceable future. Those who are protected by "things" are the least ready for the new era and are hostile to it.

✠   ✠   ✠

✦ A WARNING:

  ✦ Any serious, in-depth, personal inquiry into transcendent, or universal, or spiritual values will mean:

    ✦ A realignment of your personal relationships.
    ✦ A realignment of your family life.
    ✦ A realignment of your career.
    ✦ A reassessment of your own history.
    ✦ Interim pain, grief, and restlessness.
    ✦ Increased tension between what is and what might be in your life.
    ✦ Increased isolation from the cultural mainstream.

✠   ✠   ✠

For a series of sessions on zero-base living: a simple design for transcendent spirituality.

  ✦ Zero-base living is like:

    ✦ A woman who wakens to a sharp pain in her shoulder and remarks to herself how good it is to be able to feel at all. Without moving she gradually surveys the rest of her limbs and finds pain in only two places, her right hip and left shoulder. She moves her arm to reposition her left shoulder, then calmly rests in that position and feels the pain displaced by comfort. Delighted with the developments in her life that morning, she phones her best friend to share her joy.

✧ Zero-base living is like:

> ✧ A man who starts a business and hires his schoolmates and friends to work for him. He nourishes the business to great success and then sells it to a conglomerate, which promises not to terminate any of the current workers. Six months later, the conglomerate closes the business and terminates all the employees without notice. The former business owner, devastated by the turn of events, hires a lawyer and divides all his assets equally with all his old schoolmates and friends.

✧ Zero-base living is like:

> ✧ Tom Dixon, my legally blind albino mentor, was also handicapped by crippling arthritis. Undaunted, he was delighted to be able to see shapes and forms, and even more joyous that the shapes and forms were in Technicolor. He came to perceive that his seeing friends' normal eyesight often distracted them from seeing the true nature of the matter at hand.

✧ Zero-base living is like:

> ✧ Uncle Norman Borden who loved his life, his wife, his children, and bowling in that order. In retirement he spent many happy hours at the

alleys—hours made more delightful for him because of the company of his wife, who, though not so good a bowler, made up for her lack of skill in unblemished and exuberant enthusiasm for the game. Over the course of years, he developed a disease of the eyes called macular degeneration in which dead-on vision is diminished. A widening circle of blindness left him more and more reliant on his decreasing peripheral vision. His inability to see the pins at the other end of the alley did not much effect his score as he relied more and more on what he was able to see—a narrow band of scenery at each shoulder. When he hadn't bowled a strike, his wife reported the numbers of the pins still standing. He made fine adjustments according to his side view and, more often than not, was able to get everything but a seven-ten split. Norman also liked to travel and explore new countries and cities. People who did not know him were confused at his constant interest in the scenery to the left and right. Aunt Emily sometimes explained that he wasn't so much interested in what was to the side as he was in knowing what was ahead. Their visit to the Sistine Chapel was more strange because he tilted his head toward the floor to look up at the ceiling.

✧ Zero-base living is like:

✧ The man whose wife, never a very pleasant creature, suddenly announced that although she thought she had loved him she had, very emphatically, never liked him. She simultaneously declared that their thirty-year marriage was at an end. Being a generous and foolish man, he gave all of his assets to her so that she would have no "worries." Living on his salary was not difficult, but when his company was bought out and he was cashiered out of his job, unemployment compensation didn't cover all of his expenses. By the time he faced up to the fact that he was fifty-eight years old and was never again going to be employed at much more than minimum wage, he was living in a cheap hotel and was forced to declare bankruptcy. Once free of his debts, he called his best friend, who had been best man at his wedding, who lived across the country, to report that he had never been happier in his life because by losing all his worldly goods he had found real friends, most of whom lived in the hotel and ate together every night at the tavern downstairs.

✦ Zero-base living is like:

  ✦ Stephen Hawking
  ✦ Lou Gehrig
  ✦ Mohandas K. Ghandi
  ✦ Francis of Assisi
  ✦ Henri Nouwen
  ✦ Who else?

✠ ✠ ✠

✦ It's been my impression that we all come into the world as children who want love, and if we can't get love, we settle for power. On a personal level, once power becomes the ruling archetype in a man's or woman's psyche, that person's choices are made to achieve position, keep power, look good, and be in control.

Jean Shinoda Bolen, *Gods In Everyman: A New Psychology of Men's Lives and Loves*, HarperCollins, (Reissue paper) 1990.

✠   ✠   ✠

❖ You might like to spend some circle time, sharing the ways in which you have sought to achieve position, keep power, look good, and be in control.

✠   ✠   ✠

❖ Get the excellent study book, *Say this to the Mountain: Mark's Story of Discipleship*, and use it for a series of Jesus Circle sessions. Pay particular attention to the exercises suggested in the appendices.

✠   ✠   ✠

❖ Thanksgiving.

  ❖ If you can move, be thankful.
  ❖ If you can crawl, be more thankful.
  ❖ If you can walk, be more thankful.
  ❖ If you can run, be more thankful.
  ❖ If you can dance, be more thankful.

  ❖ If you can see black and white, be thankful.
  ❖ If you can see shape, be more thankful.
  ❖ If you can see depth, be more thankful.
  ❖ If you can see Technicolor, be more thankful.

✠   ✠   ✠

❖ Three ways to live:

1. Pretend you are immortal or have a life span stretching into a future with no horizon.
2. Concentrate all your energy on preparing for a more "meaningful and eternal life" after this mortal life ends.
3. Live as though life will end in the very next moment, or, if not that, tonight.

✧ Jesus taught the third way. "The domain of God is here, now, in your midst."

> I seek to live the third way. Consider the lilies, my friends. Wallow in the daffodils. Exult in the dew. Celebrate your sometimes-searing connections with the holiness of everything and everyone. When someone has by chance moved into the place of holy wisdom, pray that no force of evil take that from them. (Anon.)

✠ ✠ ✠

✧ Identify and share with your circle: The most oppressive domination system I live with every day is . . .

✧ Follow-up sessions might focus on identifying the common characteristics: how to cope, how to subvert, how to be a liberator from within the domination system.

✠ ✠ ✠

✧ Identify and share what ideas, notions, adages, sayings, and truths have most impeded your freedom to live abundantly.
✧ What would happen if you turned those ideas, notions, adages, sayings, and truths on their heads?

✠   ✠   ✠

✧ A View of Jesus

It distills out like this for me. Jesus' chief characteristic is outrageous courage. Since there is no God in the traditional sense, though he may have thought there was, the source of his courage is in his personal history. He was a kid raised with the prevailing notion that he was OK (in capital letters)—not OK meaning better than he was, not OK meaning in spite of being worse than he was, but OK as he was.

Imagine that as a boy or young man Jesus had a very serious illness. Then imagine that the psychological and cultural dimensions of that experience are presented in the story of his baptism and his desert experience. The result is an episode like that which is foundational for any Native American traditional shaman. Jesus has gone through the gates of death, has come back, and fears no evil or death. Then add in the data that says he was an outcast from birth, the illegitimate stepson of a tekton. He is a man who has nothing to lose. He matures into a shamanistic healer with no fear of the power of the elites oppressing him and his people.

So he takes on a nonviolent campaign to sabotage the stories, structures, and the divine laws that validate oppression. He takes on the entire domination system and creates a small community of followers who live as though the powerful elites were naked mannequins. The mannequins hate that and kill him. He didn't die then though. He died in 312 CE when the empire of Rome officially took over the churches.

✠   ✠   ✠

❖ "The dominant values of American life—affluence, achievement, appearance, power, competition, consumption, individualism— are vastly different from anything recognizably Christian."[47] Borg, Marcus, *Jesus: A New Vision: Spirit, Culture, and the Life of Discipleship.*

✠   ✠   ✠

❖ We must have profound respect for the victims of oppressive ideas and systems and move to them with healing energy along with a profound disrespect for their oppressors.

✠   ✠   ✠

❖ Use John Dominic Crossan's book, *The Essential Jesus: Original Sayings and Earliest Images,*[48] and select one saying. Then using as many rounds as the allotted time allows, attempt to understand it in the context of the oppressive culture of first-century, Roman-dominated, Jewish Palestine. Then attempt to create an analogous saying for our culture.

✠   ✠   ✠

❖ Focus a Jesus Circle session on a chapter from *The Gospel of Jesus*[49] prepared by Robert Funk and the scholars of the Jesus Seminar.

✠   ✠   ✠

[47]   Borg, Marcus J., *Jesus: A New Vision: Spirit, Culture, and the Life of Discipleship,* (San Francisco, Harper & Row, 1991).

[48]   Crossan, John Dominic, *The Essential Jesus: Original Sayings and Earliest Images,* (Edison, NJ: Castle Books, 1994).

[49]   Funk, Robert W. and the Jesus Seminar, *The Gospel of Jesus,* (Santa Rosa: Polebridge Press).

✧ "Through these rituals we remember and recommit ourselves to
the powerful example of Jesus' nonviolent witness to the
compassionate Spirit of God reflected in his public ministry of
exposing oppressive systems, in his inclusive table practice of
shared meals, and in his vision of an alternative order rooted in
justice in which all would be fed. By sharing a meal communally
or by receiving Communion together, we celebrate the nonviolent
presence of God in daily bread and express our commitment to
be in solidarity with those who hunger for real food and spiritual
nourishment.

✧ We can preserve the tradition linking a community meal with the
betrayal of Jesus by communicating clearly that Communion is a
solidarity meal in which we declare God's intent and our
commitment that all be fed. Communion should always be
understood as a risky, subversive act. It challenges systems that
accept hunger as an acceptable cost of progress. It is in food and
drink offered equally to everyone that the presence of God and
Jesus is found. But food and drink are the material bases of life, so
the Lord's Supper is a political criticism and economic challenge
as well as a sacred rite."[50]

✠   ✠   ✠

✧ I see the historical Jesus as thoroughly consumed in the
religious/political concerns of his own time and place. As such
he offers to us the role of spirit-persons whose focus is not on
some mystified domain (basileia) beyond time or the material
world that we must simply learn to see and appreciate to have a
full life. Rather, Jesus offers us a life like his, focused on a new
domain of God which is nascent here and now and ready to
emerge. The new domain is characterized by distributive justice.
It requires dedicated human agents to make it real and actual in

---

50   Nelson-Pallmeyer, Jack, *Jesus against Christianity: Reclaiming the Missing
Jesus*, (Harrisburg: Trinity Press International, 2001)

the human community. When the responsibilities to bring about the new domain are not met, there are serious consequences that fall most heavily on the most vulnerable people. Slightly edited from a post by Harry Coverston on HODOS, a Yahoo! e-group sponsored by the FaithFutures Foundation.

✠　　✠　　✠

✧ Jesus, in short, abhors both passivity and violence. He articulates, out of the history of his own people's struggles, a way by which evil can be opposed without being mirrored, the oppressor resisted without being emulated, and the enemy neutralized without being destroyed. Those who have lived by Jesus' words—Leo Tolstoy, Mohandas Gandhi, Muriel Lester, Martin Luther King, Jr., Dorothy Day, Cesar Chavez, Hildegard and Jean Goss-Meyer, Mairead (Corrigan) Maguire, Adolfo Perez-Esquivel, Daw Aung San Suu Kyi, and countless others less well known—point us to a new way of confronting evil whose potential for personal and social transformation we are only beginning to grasp today. Wink, Walter, *The Powers That Be: Theology for a New Millennium,* (New York: Galilee-Random House, 1999), p.111.

APPENDIX 1

Old Testament Violence

The following passages are the result of a quick scan. A thorough reading of the Pentateuch focused on seeing and hearing the violence therein will be distressing indeed. Especially so since much of the violence is either at the hands of God or sanctioned by God.

Exodus 19:9 ff. (Jahweh protects his abode on Mount Sinai.)

> When Moses had told the words of the people to the LORD, the LORD said to Moses: "Go to the people and consecrate them today and tomorrow. Have them wash their clothes and prepare for the third day, because on the third day the LORD will come down upon Mount Sinai in the sight of all the people. You shall set limits for the people all around, saying, 'Be careful not to go up the mountain or to touch the edge of it. Any who touch the mountain shall be put to death. No hand shall touch them, but they shall be stoned or shot with arrows; whether animal or human being, they shall not live.'"

Exodus 31:1 ff. (Through Moses, Jahweh gives his command to kill the inhabitants of the Promised Land.)

When Moses had finished speaking all these words to all Israel, he said to them: "I am now one hundred twenty years old. I am no longer able to get about, and the LORD has told me, 'You shall not cross over this Jordan.' The LORD your God himself will cross over before you. He will destroy these nations before you, and you shall dispossess them. Joshua also will cross over before you, as the LORD promised. The LORD will do to them as he did to Sihon and Og, the kings of the Amorites, and to their land, when he destroyed them. The LORD will give them over to you and you shall deal with them in full accord with the command that I have given to you. Be strong and bold; have no fear or dread of them, because it is the LORD your God who goes with you; he will not fail you or forsake you."

1 Samuel 15:1 ff. (Samuel conveys the command of God to execute a scorched-earth policy.)

Samuel said to Saul, "The LORD sent me to anoint you king over his people Israel; now therefore listen to the words of the LORD. Thus says the LORD of hosts, 'I will punish the Amalekites for what they did in opposing the Israelites when they came up out of Egypt. Now go and attack Amalek, and utterly destroy all that they have; do not spare them, but kill both man and woman, child and infant, ox and sheep, camel and donkey.'"

2 Samuel 4:12 ff. (David, the glorified shepherd king of Israel, continues the tradition.)

So David commanded the young men, and they killed Rechab and his brother, Baanah, the sons of Rimmon the Beerothite; they cut off their hands and feet and hung their bodies beside the pool at Hebron. But the head of Ishbaal they took and buried in the tomb of Abner at Hebron.

2 Samuel 20:14 ff. (A nice woman saves a city from destruction by beheading a rebel.)

> Sheba passed through all the tribes of Israel to Abel Beth-maacah; and all the Bichrites assembled and followed him inside. Joab's forces came and besieged him in Abel Beth-maacah; they threw up a siege ramp against the city, and it stood against the rampart. Joab's forces were battering the wall to break it down. Then a wise woman called from the city, "Listen! Listen! Tell Joab, 'Come here, I want to speak to you.'" He came near her; and the woman said, "Are you Joab?" He answered, "I am." Then she said to him, "Listen to the words of your servant." He answered, "I am listening." Then she said, "They used to say in the old days, 'Let them inquire at Abel'; and so they would settle a matter. I am one of those who are peaceable and faithful in Israel; you seek to destroy a city that is a mother in Israel; why will you swallow up the heritage of the LORD?" Joab answered, "Far be it from me, far be it, that I should swallow up or destroy! That is not the case! But a man of the hill country of Ephraim, called Sheba, son of Bichri, has lifted up his hand against King David; give him up alone, and I will withdraw from the city." The woman said to Joab, "His head shall be thrown over the wall to you." Then the woman went to all the people with her wise plan. And they cut off the head of Sheba, son of Bichri and threw it out to Joab. So he blew the trumpet, and they dispersed from the city, and all went to their homes, while Joab returned to Jerusalem to the king.

Psalm 21:8 ff. (A worshipful hymn conveying encouraging words from Jahweh.)

8   Your hand will find out all your enemies; your right hand will find out those who hate you.

9   You will make them like a fiery furnace when you appear. The LORD will swallow them up in his wrath, and fire will consume them.

10   You will destroy their offspring from the earth, and their children from among humankind.

11   If they plan evil against you, if they devise mischief, they will not succeed.

12   For you will put them to flight, you will aim at their faces with your bows.

Jeremiah 13:8 ff. (Jeremiah conveys the murderous wrath of the Lord toward the disobedient.)

Then the word of the LORD came to me: Thus says the LORD: Just so I will ruin the pride of Judah and the great pride of Jerusalem. This evil people, who refuse to hear my order words, who stubbornly follow their own will and have gone after other gods to serve them and worship them, shall be like this loincloth, which is good for nothing. For as the loincloth clings to one's loins, so I made the whole house of Israel and the whole house of Judah cling to me, says the LORD, in that they might be for me a people, a name, a praise, and a glory. But they would not listen.

You shall speak to them this word: Thus says the LORD, the God of Israel: Every wine-jar should be filled with wine. And they will say to you, "Do you think we do not know that every wine-jar should be filled with wine?" Then you shall say to them: Thus says the LORD: I am about to fill all the inhabitants of this land—the kings who sit on David's throne, the priests, the prophets, and all the inhabitants of Jerusalem—with drunkenness. And I will dash them one against another, parents and children together, says the LORD. I will not pity or spare or have compassion when I destroy them.

APPENDIX 2

New Testament Violence

These are but a few citations from the New Testament that give evidence of the pervasive domination system and its violence. For further exercise you might read the Book of Revelation focusing on the violence in it.

Matthew 21:33 ff.

> Jesus said, "Listen to another parable. There was a landowner who planted a vineyard, put a fence around it, dug a wine press in it, and built a watchtower. Then he leased it to tenants and went to another country. When the harvest time had come, he sent his slaves to the tenants to collect his produce. But the tenants seized his slaves and beat one, killed another, and stoned another. Again he sent other slaves, more than the first; and they treated them in the same way. Finally he sent his son to them, saying, 'They will respect my son.' But when the tenants saw the son, they said to themselves, 'This is the heir; come, let us kill him and get his inheritance.' So they seized him, threw him out of the vineyard, and killed him. Now when the owner of the vineyard comes, what will he do to those tenants? They

said to him, 'He will put those wretches to a miserable death and lease the vineyard to other tenants who will give him the produce at the harvest time.'"

Mark 15:12 ff is another parable about Jesus.

Pilate spoke to the (crowd) again, "Then what do you wish me to do with the man you call the King of the Jews?" They shouted back, "Crucify him!" Pilate asked them, "Why, what evil has he done?" But they shouted all the more, "Crucify him!" So Pilate, wishing to satisfy the crowd, released Barabbas for them, and after flogging Jesus, he handed him over to be crucified.

Then the soldiers led him into the courtyard of the palace (that is, the governor's headquarters), and they called together the whole cohort. And they clothed him in a purple cloak; and after twisting some thorns into a crown, they put it on him. And they began saluting him, "Hail, King of the Jews!" They struck his head with a reed, spat upon him, and knelt down in homage to him. After mocking him, they stripped him of the purple cloak and put his own clothes on him. Then they led him out to crucify him.

They compelled a passerby, who was coming in from the country, to carry his cross; it was Simon of Cyrene, the father of Alexander and Rufus. Then they brought Jesus to the place called Golgotha (which means the place of a skull). And they offered him wine mixed with myrrh; but he did not take it. And they crucified him, and divided his clothes among them, casting lots to decide what each should take.

It was nine o'clock in the morning when they crucified him. The inscription of the charge against him read,

"The King of the Jews." And with him they crucified two bandits, one on his right and one on his left.

Acts 7:54 ff. (in which Luke reports on Stephen's death by stoning at the hand of vigilantes)

When they heard these things, they became enraged and ground their teeth at Stephen. But filled with the Holy Spirit, he gazed into heaven and saw the glory of God and Jesus standing at the right hand of God. "Look," he said, "I see the heavens opened and the Son of Man standing at the right hand of God!" But they covered their ears, and with a loud shout all rushed together against him. Then they dragged him out of the city and began to stone him; and the witnesses laid their coats at the feet of a young man named Saul. While they were stoning Stephen, he prayed, "Lord Jesus, receive my spirit." Then he knelt down and cried out in a loud voice, "Lord, do not hold this sin against them." When he had said this, he died.

Acts 16:17 ff. (in which Luke presents a nice story about vigilantism)

One day, as we were going to the place of prayer, we met a slave-girl who had a spirit of divination and brought her owners a great deal of money by fortune-telling. While she followed Paul and us, she would cry out, "These men are slaves of the Most High God, who proclaim to you † a way of salvation." She kept doing this for many days. But Paul, very much annoyed, turned and said to the spirit, "I order you in the name of Jesus Christ to come out of her." And it came out that very hour. But when her owners saw that their hope of making money was gone, they seized Paul and Silas and dragged them into the marketplace before the authorities. When they had brought them before the magistrates, they said,

"These men are disturbing our city; they are Jews and are advocating customs that are not lawful for us as Romans to adopt or observe." The crowd joined in attacking them, and the magistrates had them stripped of their clothing and ordered them to be beaten with rods. After they had given them a severe flogging, they threw them into prison and ordered the jailer to keep them securely. Following these instructions, he put them in the innermost cell and fastened their feet in the stocks.

2 Corinthians 11 (in which Luke "quotes" Paul on his ability to absorb abuse)

"But whatever anyone dares to boast of—I am speaking as a fool—I also dare to boast of that. Are they Hebrews? So am I. Are they Israelites? So am I. Are they descendants of Abraham? So am I. Are they ministers of Christ? I am talking like a madman—I am a better one: with far greater labors, far more imprisonments, with countless floggings, and often near death. Five times I have received from the Jews the forty lashes minus one. Three times I was beaten with rods. Once I received a stoning."

1 Peter 2:18 ff. (in which the author validates abusive elites by using Jesus as a model)

Slaves, accept the authority of your masters with all deference, not only those who are kind and gentle but also those who are harsh. For it is a credit to you if, being aware of God, you endure pain while suffering unjustly. If you endure when you are beaten for doing wrong, what credit is that? But if you endure when you do right and suffer for it, you have God's approval. For to this you have been called, because Christ also suffered for you, leaving you an example, so that you should follow in his steps.

APPENDIX 3

On African Bible Study

WARNING! Use the Bible with extreme caution.
It is shaped by the domination system and its violence.

African Bible Study was one of the first applications of the circle process I used in my work. I present it here in a format that I used twenty or more years ago. As you will see this version still uses traditional domination-system terms that I am now attempting to move beyond.

This is a simple method for powerful Bible study for small groups from three to twelve. If there are more than twelve people present, it is best to split into two groups.

Here is the format presented as a series of steps. Each step must be completed before the next step is begun. A leader or convener has the responsibility to keep the group disciplined to follow the steps. Remember that dead seriousness makes for a deadly group. The group is seated in the round or as close to the round as possible.

- The leader (or someone selected beforehand) begins with an extemporaneous prayer.[51]

---

[51]   For example: We bring here this night a deep longing of the spirit that

- Beginning with the leader/convener, each person in turn to the left tells her or his name and shares any issue that might prevent him from participating fully in the process.[52]
- The leader asks three members in succession to read the passage selected for study. Others may follow in their books if they have them. A brief silence follows each reading.
- Beginning with the person to the left of the leader/convener, each person says ONE WORD that has been evoked in him by the passage.
- Beginning with the person to the left of the leader/convener, each person speaks briefly about what the passage means to him.
- Beginning with the person to the left of the leader/convener, each person speaks briefly about what the passage has come to mean to him as a result of hearing the other members of the group.
- Silence may be kept here for a time to allow the members to consider the next question.
- Beginning with the person to the left of the leader/convener, each person responds to the question: What action then, should we take this week to live out the meaning of the passage?
- If time allows, there may be an open discussion.
- The leader/convener is responsible to see that time is allowed for the final step—prayer for one another around the circle. The prayer places a hand on the pray-ee during the prayer

we may learn from one another and grow in the struggle for truth, love, and justice. May we be aided by every movement of the spirit to love, to listen, and to speak with reverence for one another and a passion to grow into the life of Jesus. Amen.

[52] The process always moves sunwise, i.e., from right to left. If a person has an issue which prevents their being truly present, time is taken to listen further and, if necessary, all lay hands on and pray for that person.

and asks in specific ways for the pray-ee to be empowered to live, to grow, and to prevail during the week ahead.

- When all are done the leader/convener sends the group away with a prayer focused on the action decision(s) made.

BIBLIOGRAPHY

Borg, Marcus J. Jesus: *A New Vision: Spirit, Culture, and the Life of Discipleship*. San Francisco: Harper & Row,1991.

_____. *The God We Never Knew: Beyond Dogmatic Religion to a More Authentic Contemporary Faith*. San Francisco: HarperSanFrancisco, 1997.

_____. *Jesus in Contemporary Scholarship*. Harrisburg: Trinity Press International, 1994.

_____, ed. *Jesus at 2000*. Boulder, CO: Westview Press, 1997.

_____. *Meeting Jesus Again for the First Time: The Historical Jesus and the Heart of Contemporary Faith*. San Francisco: HarperSanFrancisco, 1993.

Butcher, John B. *An Uncommon Lectionary*. Santa Rosa: Polebridge Press, 2002. (A lectionary of non-canonical readings that complements the Common Lectionary.)

Cain, Marvin. *Jesus the Man: An Introduction for People at Home in the Modern World*. Santa Rosa: Polebridge Press, 1999.

Chilton, Bruce. *Rabbi Jesus: An Intimate Biography*. New York: Image Books, 2002. (Digital versions available.)

_____and Jacob Neusner. *Judaism in the New Testament: Practices and Beliefs*. New York: Routledge, 1995.

Crossan, John Dominic. *Jesus: A Revolutionary Biography*. San Francisco: HarperCollins, 1994.

_____. *The Historical Jesus: The Life of a Mediterranean Jewish Peasant*. San Francisco: HarperSanFrancisco, 1991.

_____. *The Birth of Christianity: Discovering What Happened in the Years Immediately After the Execution of Jesus*. San Francisco: HarperCollins, 1998.

_____. *The Essential Jesus: Original Sayings and Earliest Images*. Edison, NJ: Castle Books, 1994.

_____. *Who Killed Jesus?: Exposing the Roots of Anti-Semitism In the Gospel Story*. San Francisco: HarperSanFrancisco, 1995.

_____and Jonathan L. Reed. *Excavating Jesus: Beneath the Stones, Behind the Texts*. San Francisco: HarperSanFrancisco, 2001.

Cupitt, Don. *After God: The Future of Religion*. New York: Basic Books, 1997.

_____. *Reforming Christianity*. Santa Rosa: Polebridge Press, 2001.

Finkelstein, Israel and Neil Asher Silberman. *The Bible Unearthed: Archeology's New Vision of Ancient Israel and the Origin of Its Sacred Texts*. New York: The Free Press, 2001.

Funk, Robert W. *Honest to Jesus: Jesus for a New Millennium*. San Francisco: Harper Collins.

_____ and Roy W. Hoover, eds. *The Five Gospels: The Search for the Authentic Words of Jesus*. New York: Macmillan, 1995.

_____ and Bernard B. Scott, eds. *The Parables of Jesus: Red Letter Edition*. A Report of the Jesus Seminar. Santa Rosa: Polebridge Press, 1988.

_____. *A Credible Jesus*. Santa Rosa: Polebridge Press.

_____ and the Jesus Seminar. *The Parables of Jesus*. Santa Rosa: Polebridge Press, 1988.

_____ and the Jesus Seminar. *The Acts of Jesus: What Did Jesus Really Do?* San Francisco: HarperSanFrancisco, 1998.

_____ and the Jesus Seminar. *The Gospel of Jesus*. Santa Rosa: Polebridge Press, 1999.

_____and the Jesus Seminar. *The Once and Future Jesus*. Essays by Marcus Borg, John Dominic Crossan, John Shelby Spong, and others. Santa Rosa: Polebridge Press.

Geering, Lloyd. *Christian Faith at the Crossroads*. Santa Rosa: Polebridge Press.

_____. *Christianity Without God*. Santa Rosa: Polebridge Press.

_____. *The World to Come: From Christian Past to Global Future.* Santa Rosa: Polebridge Press.

_____. *Tomorrow's God.* Santa Rosa: Polebridge Press, 2000.

Herzog, William R. II. *Parables as Subversive Speech: Jesus as Pedagogue of the Oppressed.* Louisville, KY: Westminster/John Knox Press, 1994.

_____. *Jesus, Justice and the Reign of God: A Ministry of Liberation.* Louisville, KY: Westminster/John Knox Press, 2000.

Holloway, Richard (Bishop of Edinburgh). *Doubts and Loves: What is Left of Christianity?* London: Canongate Books.

_____. *Godless Morality: Keeping Religion out of Ethics.* London: Canongate Books.

Heyward, Carter. *Saving Jesus from Those Who Are Right: Rethinking What It Means to Be Christian.* Minneapolis: Fortress Press, 1999.

Horsley, Richard A. *Archaeology, History, and Society in Galilee: The Social Context of Jesus and the Rabbis.* Harrisburg: Trinity Press International, 1996.

_____ and Neil Asher Silberman. *The Message and the Kingdom: How Jesus and Paul Ignited a Revolution and Transformed the Ancient World.* Minneapolis: Fortress Press, 2002.

_____. *Bandits, Prophets, and Messiahs: Popular Movements in the Time of Jesus.* San Francisco: Harper & Row, 1988.

_____. *Jesus and the Spiral of Violence: Popular Jewish Resistance in Roman Palestine.* San Francisco: Harper & Row, 1987.

_____. *Galilee: History, Politics, People.* Harrisburg: Trinity Press International, 1996.

Johnson, Luke Timothy. *The Real Jesus: The Misguided Quest for the Historical Jesus and the Truth of the Traditional Gospels.* San Francisco: HarperSanFrancisco, January 1996.

Laughlin, Paul Alan with Glenna Jackson. *Remedial Christianity: What Every Believer Should Know About the Faith but Probably Doesn't.* Santa Rosa: Polebridge Press.

Kegan, Robert. *In Over Our Heads: The Mental Demands of Modern Life.* Cambridge: Harvard University Press, 1994.

Mack, Burton L. *Who Wrote the New Testament?: The Making of the Christian Myth*. San Francisco: HarperSanFrancisco, 1995.

_____. *The Lost Gospel: The Book of Q and Christian Origins*. San Francisco: HarperCollins, 1993.

Malina, Bruce J. *Windows on the World of Jesus: Time Travel to Ancient Judea*. Louisville, KY: Westminster/John Knox Press, 1993.

_____. *The Social Gospel of Jesus: The Kingdom of God in Mediterranean Perspective*. Minneapolis: Fortress Press, 2001.

_____. *The New Testament World: Insights from Cultural Anthropology*, Third Edition. Louisville, KY: Westminster/John Knox Press, 2001.

Meier, John P. *A Marginal Jew: Rethinking the Historical Jesus*.

_____. *The Roots of the Problem and the Person*, Volume 1. New York: Doubleday, 1991.

_____. *Mentor, Message, and Miracles*, Volume 2. New York: Doubleday, 1994.

_____. *Companions and Competitors*, Volume 3. New York: Anchor Books, 2001.

Miller, Robert J., ed. *The Complete Gospels: the Scholars Version*. San Francisco: HarperSanFrancisco, 1994.

Myers, Ched et al. *Say to this Mountain: Mark's Story of Discipleship*. Maryknoll: Orbis Books, 1996.

Nelson-Pallmeyer, Jack. *Jesus Against Christianity: Reclaiming the Missing Jesus*. Harrisburg: Trinity Press International, 2001.

_____. *Is Religion Killing Us: Violence in the Bible and the Koran*. Harrisburg: Trinity Press International, 2003.

Patterson, Stephen J. *The God of Jesus: The Historical Jesus and the Search for Meaning*. Harrisburg: Trinity Press International, 1998.

Riley, Gregory J. *One Jesus, Many Christs: How Jesus Inspired Not One True Christianity, but Many*. San Francisco: HarperSanFrancisco, 1997.

Sanders E. P. *The Historical Figure of Jesus*. Penguin USA (Paper), Reprint edition, 1996.

_____. *Jesus and Judaism*. Minneapolis: Fortress Press, 1987.

Scott, Bernard Brandon. *Re-Imagine the World: An Introduction to the Parables of Jesus*. Santa Rosa: Polebridge Press.

Spong, John Shelby. *Why Christianity Must Change or Die: A Bishop Speaks to Believers in Exile*. San Francisco: HarperSanFrancisco, 1998.

Stark, Rodney. *The Rise of Christianity: How the Obscure, Marginal Jesus Movement Became the Dominant Religious Force in the Western World in a Few Centuries*. San Francisco: HarperCollins (Paper), 1997.

Taussig, Hal. *Jesus Before God: The Prayer Life of the Historical Jesus*. Santa Rosa: Polebridge Press, 1999.

Vermes, Geza. *The Changing Faces of Jesus*. Viking Press, 2001.

————. *Jesus the Jew: A Historian's Reading of the Gospels*. Minneapolis: Fortress Press, 2003.

————. *The Religion of Jesus the Jew*. London: SCM, 1993, Minneapolis: Fortress Press, 2003.

Waetjen, Herman C. *A Reordering of Power: A Socio-Political Reading of Mark's Gospel*. Minneapolis: Fortress Press, 1975.

Wink, Walter. *The Powers That Be: Theology for a New Millennium*. New York: Galilee-Random House, 1999.

On Circles

Andrews, Cecile. *The Circle of Simplicity: Return to the Good Life*. San Francisco: HarperCollins, 1997.

Baldwin, Christina and Colleen M. Kelley, illus. *Calling the Circle: The First and Future Culture*. New York: BantamBooks, 1998.

Bolen, Jean Shinoda. *The Millionth Circle: How to Change Ourselves and the World*. Berkeley: Conari Press, 1999.

Garfield, Charles, Cindy Spring and Sedonia Cahill. *Wisdom Circles: A Guide to Self-Discovery and Community Building in Small Groups*. New York: Hyperion, 1998.

Storm, Hyemeyohsts. *Seven Arrows*. New York: Ballantine Books, 1972.

Weltfish, Gene. *The Lost Universe: Pawnee Life and Culture*. Lincoln: Nebraska University Press, 1965.

Zimmerman, Jack M. *The Way of Council*. Ojai, CA: Bramble Books, 1997.

World Wide Web Resources

http://www.faithfutures.org/—Faithfutures Foundation: working together for the future of faith. A wealth of resources including the Jesus Database and advanceWORD.

http://www.tcpc.org/apr.htm—The Alliance for Progressive Religion is an informal partnership of organizations committed to providing resources and networking opportunities in the area of liberal/progressive religion.

http://www.earlygospels.net—Jesus of Nazareth in Early Christian Gospels.

http://home.epix.net/~miser17/Thomas.html—The Gospel of Thomas Homepage.

http://www.tcpc.org/—The Center for Progressive Christianity.

http://www.intac.com/~rollins/ctm.html—Christianity for the Third Millennium

http://www.ntgateway.com/—NT Gateway, Mark Goodacre's award-winning site.

http://www.reVision.org.nz/—reVision is an international journal from New Zealand devoted to biblical and religious literacy and practice.

http://www.sofn.org.uk/—The Sea of Faith international website, based in the UK, and with links to local networks in other countries. SoF was founded by Don Cupitt.

http://SnowStarInstitute.org/—Snowstar is devoted to religious literacy and tolerance in the Canadian context.

http://westarinstitute.org/—Home of the Jesus Seminar and the Polebridge Press.

http://www.united.edu/portrait/—Cam Howard's website based on the work of Marcus Borg. It includes Borg's speaking engagements.

Other Resources

Jesus and His Kingdom of Equals. Polebridge Press. (A Sunday school curriculum based on the historical Jesus which has an accompanying video.)

POSTSCRIPT

Thousands of people over the years have helped with my thinking and writing. They helped sharpen my wit. They put up with my wild notions and suffered my experiments. They argued and laughed with me.

My friend Pete (Samuel B.) Tannahill pressed me into writing this book. Pete is one of the many church alumni who are no longer able to acquiesce to the traditional doctrines and practices of the church. Most churches betray Jesus' wisdom in a host of obfuscating doctrines and corrupting hierarchies. Many folks hang on uneasily at the fringes of congregations in order to maintain the companionship and stimulation of thoughtful and spiritually rich friends. They wonder "Is it possible for us to create a alternative community of seekers without losing our spiritual integrity? Can we develop supportive associations that carry on the rich heritage of Jesus' mission and program?" As Pete kept asking, "Where do we go from here?".

For years I had been thinking about ways to develop loving groups that do Jesus honor. As an attempt to answer Pete's question, I put things in order and wrote this book. Hopefully, it will stimulate discussion and experimentation among those who are pondering the same issues.

Cecile Andrews read most of the first draft. She gave me

encouragement and very helpful feedback. John Gallagher and Jim Turner read the manuscript. Their critique caused me to recast whole sections of the book. Greg Jenks, Executive Trustee of the Faithfutures Foundation, and Tom Jackson, Abbot of the Order of Christian Workers, were enthusiastic about the project and gave me helpful advice.

The people at St. James' Episcopal Church in San Francisco were wonderful collaborators, particularly those who met for the sermon-talk-back breakfast every Sunday. We used the circle process in many settings. We worked to perfect egalitarian leadership in our circle staff meetings. In addition to study groups and support groups, the Vestry made its decisions in a circle and the Wardens were chosen using the circle process. We went round and round until the wisdom about leadership for the coming year emerged. We used the circle process in large and small groups to ponder issues like refining our mission and rebuilding our worship space.

John Dominic Crossan, Marcus Borg, Jack Nelson-Pallmeyer, and Walter Wink are foremost among my mentors. Robert W. Funk and the Scholars of the Jesus Seminar have contributed much to my meager store of knowledge.

Without Melissa DiLeonardo, Tara DellaFranzia, Thomas McAteer and Kristin Maurer, who have guided the book through the production process at Xlibris, I would have floundered badly.

I am deeply grateful to you all.